BE YE TRANSFORMED

*THE STEPS TO SPIRITUAL TRANFORMATION
REVISED AND UPDATED VERSION*

PASTOR DAVID AMOAH

First published in 2013 by
In The Way Publishing© Ltd, London

©Text 2012 David Amoah
Second edition with amendments published by
Life and Success Meddia Publishing, 2015
©Text 2012 David Amoah

The rights of David Amoah to be identified as author of this work have been asserted by him in accordance with the Copyright, Designs and Patents Acts 1988.

All rights reserved. No part of this publication may be reproduced, stored in a retrieval system or transmitted, in any form or by any means, electronic, mechanical or otherwise, without the prior written permission of the publisher.

ISBN: 978-1-907402-75-3

This book is sold subject to the condition that it may not be resold or otherwise issued except in its original binding.
The CIP catalogue record for this book is available from the British Library. British Library Cataloguing-in-Publishing Data.

All quotations are from the Holy Bible New International version and the New King James version unless otherwise stated.

Design: MIA Design
Editor: Mandi Gomez

DEDICATION

Once again I dedicate this wonderful book to the late Apostle V. O. Boafo, a former Mission director and Minister of the Apostolic Church of Ghana USA, who had a great impact on my Christian Life

CONTENTS

Foreword vii

Preface ix
   A Personal Journey ....
   My Journey is Your Journey ....
   My Life in Salvation ....

Introduction 1

The Steps or Stages of Mankind
Stage Zero: Sinners Stage 15
   How did man become sinful? 17
   Biblical References 23
   Definition of Sin and Death 24

Stage One: Repentance Stage 39
   Salvation is for everyone 45
   How to be born again 54

Stage Two: Christian Growth 91
   How can I grow as a Christian? 100

Stage Three: Soul Winning
   Preaching or Witnessing 145

Stage Four: The Ultimate 175
To study, meditate and practice the word of God

Renewal of Mind... 199

Conclusion... 207

Other Publications by Pastor David Amoah...... 213

FOREWORD

I am deeply honoured to have been asked to write this Foreword for Pastor David Amoah's book, a practical guide to be read by all Christians who desire to grow to their full potential in Christ.

I have known Pastor David Amoah for twenty-five years and have worked very closely with him in the Ministry, particularly in the last couple of years.

Having been a teacher of God's Word for over nine years, I have observed the energy and commitment of Pastor Amoah's teachings.

I feel blessed to have read *Be Ye Transformed*, for not only am I totally satisfied with the accuracy of the scripture cited herein but also confident that the way in which the book is organised will benefit even the average reader.

Moreover, let the reader remember that this is not a work of fiction or book to read at leisure or for amusement, but a work for practical study from which the reader will benefit immensely by learning how to put into practice God's Word.

This book demonstrates the true Ministry of Pastor Amoah, a genuine teacher of God's Word and a true and honest Pastor and Radio Evangelist. Pastor David Amoah has written a practical guide that illustrates how to grow in the Lord. *Be Ye Transformed* is a self-help manual that is informed by Pastor Amoah's inimitable humility and sense of humour.

Godfred Peter Obeng
General Overseer, Harvestime Ministries International

A PREFACE

A Personal Journey

This book is the result of my personal journey to Christ, and relates how I have responded to the Great Commission. First, let me share with you briefly, how I came to Christ and tell you a bit about my life after salvation.

One faithful Sunday morning in 1975 at Morso in the Asante Akim District of Ghana, West Africa, I decided to visit a friend, Wilberforce, with another best friend of mine, Oware, rather than go to church; although I had been brought up in a church, I can confess that I was not born again at that time. While we were at Wilberforce's house a messenger arrived for him, sent by his parents, to say that the Pastor of The Apostolic church, of which the parents of this friend were founding members, was going to baptise people so my friend should come to church immediately so that he would be baptised with others.

The news interested me and the other friend with whom I was with instantly, so we both decided to go with our friend and see him being baptised. Arriving there, we saw that only a few elderly people made up the congregation. The Pastor, understandably, was very happy to see us as virtually no young people belonged to the church at the time except Wilberforce who did not go to church regularly and few others. The Pastor and his helpers quickly placed a bench at the front of the church and requested that all those who wanted to be baptised should come forward and sit on the bench. My friend went up and sat on the bench.

The Pastor looked at me and my other friend and said, "What about you young boys?" I replied quickly that we were not there to be baptised ourselves but had come with our friend to see him being baptised. Patiently the Pastor continued to tell us about Christ's salvation and the need for it. In fact, to tell you the truth, I don't even know the exact words or quotation he used that day. One thing I have never forgotten is that, as he was speaking, I just interrupted him with a question: "How much do you charge for your baptismal certificate?" because baptismal certificate was chargeable at that time. To my relief, he said the money which was at the same range of the little money I had saved at that time. I then went and sat on the bench while my other friend followed. We were asked to speak out, as we repeated after the Pastor as we received and confessed Christ as our Lord and Saviour. During this time, no one in my family, including my parents, knew what was happening. In fact, they did not even know where I was at that time.

At the end of the service, we were asked to go home quickly and get ourselves a pair of shorts, a top and a towel for the baptism, which we did in no time. The most difficult aspect for me was being asked to join the parade that consisted of only a few elderly people and my friends; this procession we were expected to join, marching and singing through the centre of the town, towards the river for the baptism. My head was bowed all the way, because I felt embarrassed that other people would see me among a congregation dubbed "an old people's church" not knowing that that day and that experience was the turning point of my life. I was terribly uncomfortable for a number of hours and then finally my friends and I, along with some elderly people from the church, were baptised. To be honest, the whole time I did not know what I was doing. And another truth is that since that day the LORD has set me on a new journey that has changed my life for good. The Bible became my Number One friend after that faithful day; my whole life became centred on the Lord and things of God. I found that I could no longer tolerate the ungodly things I used to enjoy, as now I had become a new man. What inspires me most is the fact that the LORD saved me when I was in my teens, at a time when I could have been exposed to many dangers.

Now immediately after being born again, with no training or any strong foundation, I could not hide the joy I felt. Instantly, I began sharing my faith with others, preaching the Gospel and inviting people to Christ who had saved me. I had the support of the Elders of the church at that time, so I led prayer meetings and "watch-night prayer meetings". My favourite services were the crusades and dawn broadcasts, which were regularly held in my town by the church.

To the Glory of God, before we realised it, the church, which had once been dubbed "an old people's church", became a young people's church; it became the most attractive church in the town with the most youthful congregation. The scene of people responding to altar calls after preaching occupies a dominant presence in my memory. The experience of this response from the people became more pronounced when we sang songs such as:

> "Jesus is passing this way ..."
> "Come to Jesus, come to Jesus ..."

We used to sing another song in Twi, a Ghanaian language, which translates to English like this:

> He is calling you, brother,
> He is calling you,
> Listen to your God for He is calling you
> Don't delay, He is calling you
> Listen to your God for He is calling you.

My zeal to see people saved has meant that many people have come to know Christ through my invitation and personal Evangelism. At first, I was young in the Lord. Without much experience, I was not even an Officer in my church. Nevertheless, the Lord, through the Holy Spirit, used me to transform the lives of many who came to know Christ through me.

In the early days, my witnessing was extensive and became a feature everywhere I went, particularly when I was travelling long distances. I would travel in what are known in Ghana as "passenger cars", which are large people carriers that take a great number of passengers. This created the opportunity for me to preach to as many people as possible about Christ who had saved me.

I would position myself in the back or front seat, and immediately the driver had moved off, I would stand up and begin to preach. To my advantage, at that time, one could start preaching in such places without having to ask permission from anybody.

On one of these occasions, something happened that I could never forget. I had been preaching over some great distance, from Konongo to Kumasi in the Ashanti Region, and after, because of the power of my preaching, some passengers began giving me offerings although I had not asked for any. I could already sense the impact of my message when, at the end of this journey, one elderly man who had been listening to me preaching, came up to me and said: "Well done young man, thanks for your wonderful message; that was good. Could you give me the Bible quotation you used so I can read it when I get home?"

I was a young believer at the time with a lot less experience and only elementary knowledge about God's word. I had no idea that the quotation I had just quoted, which was about Noah and the Flood, was not in fact from the Bible, but taken from something I had heard people saying.

The reality was that the Noah and the Flood story as I had just been preaching it was not from the Bible; but I got out my Bible anyway and started to look for the quotation in the book of Genesis. Surely, I thought, I was bound to find the story about the Flood. Of course, I could not find the "passage" from which I had just quoted.

To my relief, while I was thumbing through the pages in Genesis, the old man pulled out a piece of paper and a pen and wrote his address on it. He then gave me the piece of paper with some money and said, "Take it, if at any time you find that quotation, please post it to me." At this time, I was totally wet from head to toe with sweat, as the heat of my embarrassment was complimented by a very hot and sunny day.

That day was the most uncomfortable experience in my Evangelistic life. However, I was not discouraged in my passion to share my faith with others, and to bring them to Christ. I was rather encouraged by this important lesson, to the extent that ever since, I have never repeated or quoted anything in my sermons unless I am sure it is in the Bible. It has been many years now, and with great joy I am still preaching and inviting people to Christ. Praise God!

My Journey is Your Journey

The point I am trying to make here is that you could face similar challenges. Perhaps it could be an even bigger obstacle, but don't be discouraged by anything, not even the mistakes you make. God will honour your commitments to bring souls to Him. He said, "If I am lifted up I will bring up souls to myself." So stop making excuses by saying that you are not a Pastor, an Elder or an Officer of the church. Remember that your invitation is as valid as the next person's, and know that your invitation will make a real difference to somebody's life.

In Ephesians (2:10) it says that we were saved so that we could do good work for Him: consider a tree without fruit; it is useless because it bears no fruit.

So ask yourself, "What am I doing?"

Then do something now, as it says in John (15:16) "you were saved so that you could bring others to God."

I find it very sad sometimes that some believers do not even invite people to their church. They do not invite those who are even closer than we are to Christ, by this I mean, more or less, the "man on the street". Worst of all are those, like the king in Naaman's story, that instead of bringing people to Christ seem bent on driving people away, an act Jesus warns us against, when He says in (Matthew 18:6):

"But if anyone causes one of these little ones who believe in me to sin, it would be better for him to have a large millstone hung around his neck and to be drowned in the depths of the sea."

Friends, this is very serious warning from the master, and my advice to you is that if you are unable to bring people to Him, which would indeed be very good on your part, please do not drive people away from Him. We will return to Naaman's story for further study later in the book.

Another reason why some believers fail to bring or invite people to Christ is that often we are unable to let go of our "old man". Consider the Samaritan woman who left behind her water jar and then ran to the city. Now let me tell you that the water bottle, here, in this story is symbolic of her "old nature". What is this saying? It indicates that the nature of our invitation can determine the response. I believe the Samaritan woman went into the city as a new person having dropped the old person. So be serious and be convinced in your invitation. Leave your jar behind. What I mean is to leave behind anything that might hold you back, anything that might stop you from running into the city. Some things from your past may be a great hindrance to your witnessing unless you drop them. So drop them and forget them.

As you read this book, I advise you as a fellow believer to leave behind anything that might hinder you from feeling free to testify to others about Christ who has saved you and all of us, so that we will also come to know Him and partake in His freely given salvation.

Remember what the author of the book of Hebrews says: "therefore, since we are surrounded by such a great cloud of witnesses, let us throw off everything that hinders and the sin which so easily entangles, and let us run with perseverance the race marked out for us." (Hebrews 12:1)

The problem for many in dropping what hinders them is the question: how can I do it? My advice to you once again is this: it is not you but Him; the problem and the solution lies in your availability, so just rely on the Holy Spirit who is ready to help you to witness. Paul said, "Not that we are competent in ourselves to claim anything for ourselves, but our competence comes from God. He has made us competent as ministers of a new covenant – not of the letter but of the Spirit; for the letter kills, but the Spirit gives life." (2 Corinthians 3:5–6)

The Holy Spirit is always ready to help you to witness as part of His mission. Jesus said, "When the counsellor comes, whom I will send to you from the Father, the Spirit of truth who goes out from the Father, he will testify about me." (John 15:26)

My Life in Salvation

Today by the grace of God I am a senior Pastor at The Good Way Apostolic Church, Edmonton, in London; a renowned preacher and a teacher of God's word. I am also well known as a radio evangelist and an author, something I never dreamed I would do in my life. To God is the Glory: when I preach on the radio, listeners call in with feedback about the messages they have just heard, some screaming live on air in excitement, while others talk in convicted, trembling voices.

To the Glory of Him who gives me the grace and the ability; these listeners often tell me how they have been blessed by my message; how it has changed their lives; how deeply my message has touched them; and how "to-the-point!" and personal a topic has been for them. During my radio programmes, I have even received calls – on several occasions in fact – from people of other religions, especially Muslims, claiming to have been touched by the word of God during my programme. The most fulfilling experience of all is when listeners call to say that they were on the point of suicide, but having received comfort and encouragement from my message, they have regained hope and changed their minds, Halleluiah!

Praise God! I tell you all this for the Glory of God, not to boast, I do so to Glorify the LORD. He has made everything possible for me, so that you will also be encouraged. God can use anyone who avails himself to accomplish great things. What could be more fulfilling in my life than to hear the kinds of testimonies I have shared with you previously? But don't forget, this is the experience while witnessing about Christ. The good news is that I know the Lord still has not finished with me yet! I no longer preach in passenger cars as I used to thirty-five years ago, now people listen to me on a local radio station in London and worldwide via the internet. The greatest testimony of all is that through my messages people respond to the call of God. People are being saved every day when I preach. Hallelujah!

Those who live near our church often join us because they have heard my radio preaching. Others who are already born again, and, therefore, regularly go to church, they are also growing in the Lord through my preaching and teaching of God's word. I tell you all this to encourage you – never, ever allow anything or anyone to discourage or hinder you when you respond to the Great Commission to bring people to Christ. Although it may be a struggle at first, as you grow in Christ and bring people to Him, the Lord God will bless you, because you made yourself available.

Remember what Paul said in 1 Corinthians (1:26–29):

"Brothers, think of what you were when you were called. Not many of you were wise by human standards; not many were influential; not many were of noble birth. But God chose the foolish things of the world to shame the wise; God chose the weak things of the world to shame the strong. He chose the lowly things of this world and the despised things – and the things that are not – to nullify the things that are, so that no one may boast before him."

INTRODUCTION

As a preacher and teacher of God's word, I believe that through the Scriptures and my personal journey in life, I have identified the following five steps or stages in a man's life. I believe every man and every woman on the face of this earth must go through these steps or stages, irrespective of whom they are or where they come from—rich or poor, black or white, believer or non-believer—whether or not we are aware of it. These steps and stages must be taken by everyone on his or her way through life, towards heaven for believers, and hell for non-believers.

To be transformed all believers should go through all the stages described below; it is for this purpose that I am writing this book, but believe it or not, many believers, due to ignorance and lack of faith in the word of God, do not attain most of these stages. Some will remain babies, unable to grow even after they are born again. Others may not even reach Stage Four – which I call the Ultimate Stage – and which is to know through reading or listening, meditation, and by practicing the word of God.

Because of this, many believers even though they will go to heaven, will miss their inheritance here on earth as children of God. Non-believers, on the other hand, will remain at Stage Zero until they go to hell, if they fail to progress through to repentance stage. Below are the stages we are about to discuss, the five steps or stages of your transformation, which are:

1. **Stage Zero:** the unsaved, non-believers, sinners' stage
2. **Stage One:** the repentant, who have received Christ; the born again stage
3. **Stage Two:** the Christian growth stage
4. **Stage Three:** the soul-winning stage
5. **Stage Four:** the Ultimate Stage

The good news about these stages is that, at every step, there is a chance and a real will for everyone to progress to the next stage, until finally one reaches Stage Four: the Ultimate Stage. It is very important to note that everyone is given the opportunity or will to choose his or her final destination.

At each of these stages, the Lord God in His infinite love and wisdom gives us the opportunity and the will to succeed: why and how will be explained in more detail in the next chapter. To succeed, one will need God's assistance through the Holy Spirit, together with the support of faithful men who are obediently responding to their Evangelistic Ministry, the Great Commission, which will help you to grow or progress to the next stage if you are ready to do so. On other hand, failure to grow or progress at any of the stages outlined above can result in one or some of the following:

1. Doomed to hell are the non-believers at Stage Zero.

2. Falling away as result of trials and temptations. That is, God will test our faith for our own good, but the devil on the other hand will tempt us in order to see believers fall and non-believers go to hell.

    Jesus said (Matthew 13:20–21) "The one who received the seed that fell on the rocky places is the man who hears the word and at once receives it with joy. But since he has no root, he lasts only a short time. When trouble or persecution comes because of the word, he quickly falls away."

3. As John also teaches us, there will be a time when wolves come after sheep. Believe it or not, the devil never gives up pursuing anyone and will try to win back all the people who have progressed from Stage Zero. Just as John said, he will come after the sheep even when they are running from him; attracting them with temptations, so if real efforts are not made to progress, to resist temptation, there is a chance that even those who have progressed

from Stage Zero will fall. John 10:12–13 reminds us: "The hired hand is not the shepherd who owns the sheep. So when he sees the wolf coming, he abandons the sheep and runs away. Then the wolf attacks the flock and scatters it. The man runs away because he is a hired hand and cares nothing for the sheep." Through excuses of their own, some believers will not fulfil their duty by responding to the command of Jesus' Great Commission, "Go ye into the whole world and preach the Gospel." For more information about the tests and trails presented to us by God and the temptations that the devil puts in our way, I recommend that you read my book *Temptation*, which is the revised edition of my first book, **Lead Us Not into Temptation**.

4. By not enjoying the full benefit or blessings from God, you disregard knowledge; for no one will enjoy what he or she does not know is there for them, as the prophet said (Hosea 4:6): "My people are destroyed from lack of knowledge. Because you have rejected knowledge, I also reject you as my priests; because you have ignored the law of your God, I will also ignore your problem."

5. Some people become stagnant and fail to grow at some stages, because for them, things have become the norm and, eventually, they lose

their first love: their faith is what I am referring to here. In some cases are those who fail to progress from an alliance with the devil; they become an enemy of Christ and the church, the body of Christ, as 2 Peter 2:2 states: 'Many will follow their shameful ways and will bring the way of truth into dispute." These people begin to dispute the things they believed in previously and deny things about which previously they preached or witnessed.

Just as a child requires good food and nourishment in order to grow physically and mentally, so the same principles apply in order to progress or grow to any of the stages outlined above. It begins with salvation, progresses to the race to serve God, and then your real journey starts—transformation into a true Christian, at which point you are well on your way towards the Ultimate Stage. However, remember that the Gospel or the word of God is your spiritual food, and it is essential to feed yourself with this. Paul said in Romans 6:1, "I am not ashamed of the Gospel because it is the power of God for the salvation of everyone who believes; first the Jew, then for the Gentile [the Greeks]." The word of God has the power to change the life of everybody, irrespective of which stage they have reached.

In defending his manner of preaching, Paul wrote in his first letter to the Corinthians' Church that the word of God has the power to bring about change for the better and the salvation of mankind more than any other means.

"For the message of the cross is foolishness to those who are perishing, but to us who are being saved it is the power of God." (1 Corinthians 1:18)

The author of Hebrews also describes the word of God as a very powerful tool with which to judge the heart. He said:

"For the word of God is living and active. Sharper than any double edge sword, it penetrates dividing the soul, spirit, joints and marrow; it judges the thoughts and attitudes of the heart." (Hebrews 4:12)

Advising his readers, the apostle James says that we should not only read the word of God but obey it as well. James advised that we should do as God instructs. Reading, without obeying the word of God, brings no blessing. With this, James says that the perfect law (The word of God) gives freedom:

"But the man who looks intently into the perfect law that gives freedom, and continues to do this, not forgetting what he has heard, but doing it – he will be blessed in what he does." (James 1:25)

The word of God is the greatest tool as it leads to repentance, revealing to every man the depravity of mankind without Christ, and the necessity for repentance and regeneration. In addition, the word of God points to Jesus who will lead us all to salvation.

On your journey, it is helpful to have a mentor – an individual or a group that will support and encourage you in times of difficulty. When you need direction in the process of progressing, Paul advises (Romans 10:13–15):

"... for, everyone who calls on the name of the Lord will be saved. How then can they call on the one they have not believed in? And how can they believe in the one of whom they have not heard? And how can they hear without someone preaching to them? And how can they preach unless they are sent? As it is written, 'how beautiful are the feet of those who bring good news!'"

We all need help somewhere along the line in our Christian life until we become mature or reach the Ultimate Stage.

This is what Paul means when he says that when He ascended to heaven He gave gifts to the church:

"It was He who gave some to the apostles, some to the prophets, some to be evangelists, and some to be Pastors and teachers, to prepare God's people for works of service, so that the body of Christ may be built up until we all reach unity in the faith and in the knowledge of the Son of God and become mature, attaining to the whole measure of the fullness of Christ. Then we will no longer be infants, tossed back and forth by the waves, and blown here and there by every wind of teaching and by the cunning and craftiness of men in their deceitful scheming." (Ephesians 4:11–14)

Many times, I have told members of my church, especially those who regularly attend Bible study sessions, that they are fortunate and blessed to have me as a gift to them from God. I say to them, as we just read in the story of my salvation, that I did not have the opportunity they now have when I first came to Christ.

Although I have enjoyed some mentoring from both Pastors and Elders, I have taken inspiration from some who did not even know me. I advise my listeners not to abuse the gift, but to take advantage of it and make good use of the opportunity God has given them. They should not be like me, who at first could not approach the Pastors and Elders who were trying to offer me inspiration. I tell my listeners and the congregation that they can come to me at any time for direction or any support they may need. I thank God that I can say that with His glory many, who have remained faithful and obedient because of my teaching and support, are doing very well in the Lord.

To close Part 1, I would like to pay honourable tribute to the late Apostle V.O. Boafo, Apostle of the Apostolic Church in Ghana; may his soul rest in peace. He was a mentor to me, although he did not even know me, and was instrumental in my growth in the Lord. His intervention occurred during two testimonies, which I heard him give during two national conventions organised by The Apostolic Church in Ghana in the 1970s. These testimonies had a life-changing impact on me and I remember vowing to the Lord as I heard the second testimony: "Lord," I said, "I want to know you more, exactly as this man does".

Let me summarise both of Apostle V. O. Boafo's testimonies, as I believe they may be of interest to you. In the first testimony, he talked about how the Lord miraculously delivered him from his two attackers through speaking in tongues. The attackers struck as he was on his way to work and had wanted to rob him; they threatened to kill him if he did not give them all his money.

One of them began reciting something that sounded like Arabic, which prompted Apostle V. O. Boafo to speak in tongues because he had already been baptised by the Holy Spirit. To his surprise, the strange words attracted the attention of the people that were in the area at the time, and they rushed to the scene. The man who was speaking what sounded like Arabic began weeping and shouting very loudly, and the people who had rushed to the scene asked him why he was crying, and demanded to know what the Pastor had done to him.

According to Apostle V. O. Boafo, the robber said that it was as if someone had taken a powerful grip around his neck and was trying to kill him. Another interesting event in this story is that the other attacker, sensing that something extraordinary was happening to his colleague, took to his heels and was eventually traced to a gutter, where he lay, washed by the waste water that ran through it.

In his second testimony, Apostle V. O. Boafo testified to the power of God, which is able to turn around every circumstance. He said that one night he was bitten by a snake in his room. The snake was killed with the help of neighbours, but worse was to come, as later in hospital he was told by doctors that he would never have children because of the snakebite. Thank God, however, for when he stood and testified on the platform that day he told us that he now had "two and half children", by which he meant that he already had two children and that his wife was pregnant again. Praise God.

I would also like to take this opportunity to thank and pay tribute to my late uncle S. K. Ofosu – who during the period I am referring to was a member of the Apostolic Church in Ghana, Konongo Assembly – for his generosity. He always paid my fares to the national conventions so that I could hear these testimonies, which led me to take a vow to know and to serve God better, and which vow has transformed my life. Undoubtedly, these things have helped me to grow in my Christian life.

As you progress, it is very important to realise that at some stages particular nourishment and certain people may not be relevant; at other stages, the word, your spiritual food, will be elementary for the believer. Just as milk will nourish babies, it alone will not be sufficient for a mature person who needs solid food. Thus it is that the young Christian and a mature Christian require different spiritual nourishment.

Furthermore, in the case of mentoring, it may be necessary to leave some people or mentors behind if the way they conduct their life does not fit in with yours, and if their faith is of no further help to your progress. As I have reminded you, if you want to grow as a Christian, you must be prepared to let go of some people and some things from your life so that you may grow. If you insist on holding on to everything, you will not grow. Now let us move on to discuss the details of the steps to spiritual transformation.

THE STEPS TO SPIRITUAL TRANSFORMATION

Stage Zero: Sinners' Stage

This first stage, Stage Zero, is the point where the non-believer begins. It is the stage of sinners. Stage Zero is the result of mankind's zero-connection with God, a time without God, a time without hope and a total separation from God. This is the stage when life has become meaningless because we are disconnected from both God and Jesus who is the light of the world. At this stage, life has become dark just as when a light is turned off in a very dark room at night (John 1:1–34). As a result, all those at this stage are under the dominion of Satan, the prince of darkness. At this stage, the unsaved are blind and cannot see the things of God, all of which are spiritual. He that is unsaved is weak and cannot do anything good for himself; therefore, he needs a helper to assist him out of this situation. Man in this state is said to be natural and thus unable to understand the things of God, which are of the Spirit: "But the natural man does not receive the things of the Spirit of God, for they are foolishness to him; nor can he know them, because they are spiritually." (1 Corinthians 2:14)

In fact, although it is uncomfortable for me to say this, the truth is that every person in this world, including believers whether they are dead or alive, has found himself or herself at this stage at some point in their lives. It is the beginning for everyone, where the transformation of every one of us begins. Just remember that all of us are sinners through the sins of Adam and Eve, naturally.

When the Lord called Paul, this is what He told him: "I will rescue you from your own people and from the gentiles. I am sending you to them to open their eyes and turn them from **darkness to light** and from **the power of Satan to God**, so that they may receive forgiveness of sins and a place among those who are sanctified by faith in me." This was what Paul told Agrippa when he was asked to speak in Jesus' defence; Paul told of his own salvation and Jesus' commission when he met Him on the road to Damascus. (Acts 26:16–18)

In his letter to the Ephesians' Church, Paul describes the state of the non-believers (Ephesians 2:11–13):

"Therefore, remember that formerly you who are Gentiles by birth and called 'uncircumcised' by those who call themselves 'the circumcision' (that done in the body by the hands of men) – remember that at the time you were **separate from Christ**, excluded from citizenship in Israel and foreigners to the covenants of the promise, **without hope and without God** in the world.

But now in Christ Jesus you *who once were far away* have been brought near by the blood of Christ."

He also has this to say about believers, proving that non-believers, or those without Christ, are in darkness:

"For you were once darkness, but now you are light in the Lord. Live as children of light …" (Ephesians 5:8)

"But you are a chosen people, a royal priesthood, a holy nation, a people belonging to God, that you may declare the praises of him who called you out of darkness into his wonderful light. Once you were not a people, but now you are the people of God; once you had not received mercy, but now you have received mercy." (1 Peter 2:9–10)

How did man become sinful?

Man became sinful wilfully and by choice, that is, he chose to sin against the Lord his Maker. The Lord had already told Adam and Eve not to eat the fruit of the tree of good and evil; He told them they would die if they ate the fruit.

"And the Lord God commanded the man, 'You are free to eat of any tree in the garden; but you must not eat of the tree of the knowledge of good and evil, for when you eat of it you will surely die." (Genesis 2:16–17)

The scenario is very much like someone ignoring all the warning signs that point to a dangerous spot on a road, or ignoring the No Entry signs into a particular place. I remember driving into a town in the eastern region of Ghana years ago, and seeing a signpost that read "Danger Skeleton Ahead". This particular road had claimed many lives in the past, and this sign was alerting drivers to the danger that lay ahead; those who failed to react to these words of warning were likely to have an accident. Thank God that these days planners have made a diversion on this road so that drivers avoid the danger spot.

So man ignored God's warning and chose to obey Satan instead. Adam and Eve ate of the forbidden fruit:

"Now the serpent was craftier than any of the wild animals the Lord God had made. He said to the woman, 'Did God really say, "You must not eat from any tree in the garden?"

"The woman said to the serpent, 'We may eat fruit from the trees in the garden, but God did say, "You must not eat fruit from the tree that is in the middle of the garden, and you must not touch it, or you will die."

"'You will surely die', the serpent said to the woman. 'For God knows that when you eat of it your eyes will be opened, and you will be like God, knowing good and evil.'"

"When the woman saw that the fruit of the tree was good for food and pleasing to the eye, and also desirable for gaining wisdom, she took some and ate it. She also gave some to her husband, who was with her, and he ate it. Then the eyes of both of them were opened, and they realised that they were naked; so they sewed fig leaves together and made coverings for themselves." (Genesis 3:1–7)

Just as we have freedom of choice and the LORD does not interfere, so the Lord gave Adam and Eve freedom to choose what they wanted to do. Like Adam and Eve, in exercising your freedom of choice, I put before you this question: whom do you obey or listen to, is it the devil or the LORD? Note that choosing to obey the devil can only lead to destruction, but in obeying God He leads you to life.

As the result of his disobedience, man became a sinner and died. Man's relationship with God was severed when he disobeyed God's command, man had already been told: "And the God commanded the man, 'You are free to eat of any tree in the garden; but you must not eat of the tree of the knowledge of good and evil, for when you eat of it you will **surely die**.'" (Genesis 2:16–17)

Paul reiterates the message, saying: "For the wages of sin is death, but the gift of God is eternal life in Christ Jesus our Lord." (Romans 6:23)

All men naturally became sinners through the sins of Adam and Eve. While teaching on the subject of sin one day in our Bible study class, someone asked a very good question, one that I believe many other people may want to ask too. He asked: "Why do you say that all men, that is, every person born of a woman is a sinner without Christ, and also why do you say every man has been to Stage Zero?" He continued: "What about those who were born into a Christian home or born of Christian parents; these people have been going to church since they were born so how could they have been at Stage Zero?"

The answer to this question is simple and is the main point I am trying to put across in this section of the book: when Satan succeeded in tempting Adam and Eve to choose his will over God's they sinned, so sin was born into the world or into the human race. Thus, every man born of a woman after Adam and Eve has naturally inherited their sin, no matter whom you are or where you come from. Just as birds and animals produce offspring after their kind, so it is that all men are the product of the sinful nature of Adam and Eve, our parents. Birds' chicks learn to fly as they mature, just as other creatures learn to walk or crawl at a certain time, just like their parents.

Paul said to the Ephesians (Ephesians 2:1–3): "As for you, you were dead in your transgressions and sins, in which you used to live when you followed the ways of this world and of the ruler of the kingdom of the air, the Spirit who is now at work in those who are disobedient. All of us also lived among its desires and thoughts. Like the rest, we were by nature objects of wrath." Here, Paul is saying that we have all been there before, just like others (non-believers), we were all at Stage Zero at one time, and we are all sinners, because we are the descendants of Adam and Eve.

This is why even little children sometimes lie and become angry; why they commit so many transgressions although nobody has taught them to do wrong, it is natural. Clearly, therefore, every man who has lived or who is living on this earth has been at or is still at Stage Zero. All men are sinners without Christ, except Jesus who was born without sin, until He sinned in order to save mankind.

In his writings, Paul said, "For what the law was powerless to do in that it was weakened by the sinful nature, God did by sending His own Son in the likeness of sinful man to be a sinful offering. And so he condemned sin in sinful man, in order that the righteous requirements of the law might be fully met in us, who do not live according to the sinful nature but according to the Spirit." (Romans 8:3–4)

Paul also said, "God made him who had no sin to be sin for us, so that in him we might become the righteousness of God." (2 Corinthians 5:21)

And Paul tells us again: "Christ redeemed us from the curse of the law by becoming a curse for us, for it is written: 'Cursed is everyone who is hung on a tree.' He redeemed us in order that the blessing given to Abraham might come to the Gentiles through Christ Jesus, so that by faith we might receive the promise of the Spirit." (Galatians 3:13–14)

David fittingly describes himself and all men as sinners when he says, "Surely I was sinful at birth, sinful from the time my mother conceived me" (Psalm 51:5). We were all conceived by the sinful nature of our sinful parents. Notice once again, and settle it in your mind, that none of us have or ever can avoid Stage Zero; we have all been there before, but thank God for the gift of His only begotten Son, Jesus Christ, through whom salvation came to all men, through Him men could progress to Stage One.

Moses recorded that after the Flood in Noah's time, the Lord promised never to destroy the world again with a flood, even though man is sinful from his childhood. (Genesis 8:21)

And if still you are in any doubt that we are saved in Jesus, it is written: "But when the time had fully come,

God sent His Son, born of a woman, born under law, to redeem those under law, that we might receive the full rights of sons." (Galatians 4:4–5)

Biblical references to support the assertion that "All men are Sinners without Christ"

(Ecclesiastes 7:20) "There is not a righteous man on earth who does what is right and never sins."

(Isaiah 53:6) "We all, like sheep, have gone astray, each of us has turned to his own way; and the Lord has laid on him the iniquity of us all."

(Romans 3:10) "As it is written: 'There is no-one righteous, not even one …'"

(Romans 3:23) "'For all have sinned and fall short of the Glory of God …'"

(Romans 5:19) "For just as through the disobedience of the one man the many were made sinners, so also through the obedience of the one man the many will be made righteous."

(Romans 5:20) "The law was added so that the trespass might increase. But where sin increased, grace increased all the more …"

(Romans 5:21) "... So that, just as sin reigned in death, so also grace might reign through righteousness to bring eternal life through Jesus Christ our LORD."

Definition of sin and death

What is sin?

1. According to Paul: "But the man who has doubts is condemned if he eats, because his eating is not from faith; and everything that does not come from faith is sin" (Romans 14:23). What this means is that doing anything without faith, in other words doubting God, or not believing that which God has said will come true, is a sin according to Paul.

2. According to John: "Everyone who sins breaks the law, in fact, sin is lawlessness" (1 John 3:4). Failing to live by God's law or standard, which can only be measured by the word of God, is a sin.

3. Again according to John: "All wrongdoing is sin, and there is sin that does not lead to death" (1 John 5:17). Committing a crime, any bad or illegal behaviour committed against God or other people, is a sin according to John.

So you can see that Adam and Eve committed the ultimate sin by doubting what God had told them. They failed to live by God's law, and committed a sin by doing what they had been forbidden to do. In the same way, we sin against God and our neighbours when we do not do that which we know is right. Therefore, you must take note that, no matter what you think or feel, the word of God is the final authority we must all look to, and live by, if we want to avoid sin.

What is death?

The word death means separation from God: a life full of darkness and spiritual blindness. As described by the Scriptures, there are three types of death:

Spiritual Death (or spiritual separation from God)

Spiritual death is the first death experienced by man, the result of Adam and Eve's disobedience in the Garden of Eden. I believe many people are mixed up and confused about the difference between spiritual and physical death.

Remember in (Genesis 2:16–17) when the Bible says: "And the Lord God commanded the man, 'You are free to eat of any tree in the garden; but you must not eat of the tree of the knowledge of good and evil, for when you eat of it you shall surely die.'" Death, as it applies to Adam and Eve, is a spiritual death, for when they ate of the forbidden fruit, I believe, they died spiritually immediately after they had eaten it. They became separated from God, spiritually cut off from Him, although they were still alive physically.

(Romans 5:18) "Consequently, just as the result of one trespass was condemnation for all men, so also the result of one act of righteousness was justification that brings life for all men."

(Ephesians 2:1–3) "As for you, you were dead in your transgressions and sin, in which you used to live when you followed the ways of this world and of the ruler of the kingdom of the air, the Spirit who is now at work in those who are disobedient. All of us lived among them at one time, gratifying the cravings of our sinful nature and following its desires and thoughts. Like the rest, we were by nature objects of wrath."

This is the deplorable state of those at Stage Zero: they are spiritually dead in sin because they are without Christ; they are separated from God spiritually.

Physical death

Physical death is when the soul and the Spirit are separated from the body; the Bible says that it does not please God when sinners (those is Stage Zero) die. So God asks that all men should "come to repentance before they die physically." This is because there is no repentance for the sinner at Stage Zero, whether dead spiritually or physically, as we will see later in Luke's

Gospel and the story of the rich man, and the poor man, Lazarus.

We see that God pronounced the physical death of man after he had already suffered spiritual death, having been disobedient (Genesis 3:19):

"By the sweat of your brow you will eat your food until you return to the ground, since from it you were taken; for dust you are and to dust you will return."

Abel was the first man to taste physical death when he was murdered by his own brother, Cain. (Genesis 4:8)

Paul, writing to the Romans, said that just as through one man (Adam) physical death came about because of spiritual death, so also physical life is the result of spiritual life through one man – Christ:

"So that, just as sin reign in death so also grace might reign through righteousness, to bring eternal life through Jesus Christ our Lord." (Romans 5:21)

(2 Peter 3:8–9) "But do not forget this one thing, dear friends: With the Lord a day is like a thousand years, and a thousand years are like a day. The Lord is not slow in keeping his promise, as some understand slowness. He is patient with you, not wanting anyone to perish but everyone to come to repentance."

(Ezekiel 18:30–32) "'Therefore, O house of Israel, I will judge you, each one according to his ways,' declares the Sovereign LORD. 'Repent! Turn away from all your offences; then sin will not be your downfall. Rid yourselves of all the offences you have committed, and get a new heart and a new spirit. Why will you die, O house of Israel? For I take no pleasure in the death of anyone', declares the Sovereign LORD. Repent and live!'"

In fact, all human beings must face this initial or physical death when the body returns to the ground from which it came, except those who the LORD Himself chooses to take home; they do not experience physical death.

The writer of Hebrews affirms this when he says:

"Just as man is destined to die once, and after that to face judgement, so Christ was sacrificed once to take away the sins of many people; and he will appear a second time, not to bear sin, but to bring salvation to those who are waiting for him." (Hebrews 9:27–28)

But thank God that Jesus has conquered death for us so that even when we die or suffer the second death, the physical death, we are left with hope that we will rise up again to be with the Lord. "But we see Jesus, who was made a little lower than the angels, now crowned with glory and honour because he suffered death, so that by the grace of God he might taste death for everyone." (Hebrews 2:9)

Eternal death (or the second death)
As described for us in the Book of Revelation.

The Apostle John says that eternal death is the second death, when man is eternally disconnected or cut-off from God. This is when man is living eternally with God. This is when men remain at Stage Zero until they die (physical death) without progressing to Stage One by accepting Jesus Christ who is God's gift of salvation. All those in this state will remain eternally separated from God.

(Revelation 20:11–15) "Then I saw a great white throne and him who was seated on it. Earth and sky fled from his presence, and there was no place for them. And I saw the dead, great and small, standing before the throne, and books were opened. Another book was opened, which is the book of life. The dead were judged according to what they had done as recorded in the books. The sea gave up the dead that were in it, and death and Hades gave up the dead that were in them, and each person was judged according to what they have done. Then death and Hades were thrown into the lake of fire. The lake of fire is the second death. If anyone's name was not found written in the book of life, he was thrown into the lake of fire."

(Revelation 21:8) "But the cowardly, the unbelieving, the vile, the murderers, the sexually immoral, those who practise magic arts, the idolaters and all lairs their place will be the fiery lake of burning sulphur. This is the second death."

Hope for the sinner

In the sight of human beings, it may seem impossible for anyone to progress from Stage Zero, just as it may appear impossible for a dead man to run when danger is approaching. But with God, anything is possible. All things are easy in the sight of God. Everybody has the chance to progress from Stage Zero, which is why Jesus had to suffer on the cross.

With Jesus Christ, all things are possible, just as He told His disciples, having spoken to the rich young man who could not bear it when He (Jesus) told him what he could do to inherit the kingdom of God.

(Matthew 19:16–17) "Now a man came up to Jesus and asked 'Teacher, what good thing must I do to get eternal life?'

'Why do you ask me about what is good?'

Jesus replied, 'There is only one who is good. If you want to enter life, obey the commandments. No one is good but one, that is, God. But if you want to enter into life, keep the commandments.'"

(Matthew 19:18–19) "'Which ones?' the man enquired.

Jesus replied, 'Do not murder, do not commit adultery, do not steal, do not give false testimony, honour your father and mother, and love your neighbour as yourself.'"

(Matthew 19:20–21) "'All these I have kept' the young man said. 'What do I still lack?'

Jesus answered, 'If you want to be perfect, go, sell your possessions and give to the poor, and you will have treasure in heaven. Then come, follow me.'"

(Matthew 19:22–23) "When the young man heard this, he went away sad, because he had great wealth."

(Matthew 19:23–24) "Then Jesus said to his disciples, 'I tell you the truth, it is hard for a rich man to enter the kingdom of heaven. Again I tell you, it is easier for a camel to go through the eye of a needle than for a rich man to enter the kingdom of God.'"

(Matthew 19:25–26) "When the disciples heard this, they were greatly astonished and asked, 'Who then can be saved?'

Jesus looked at them and said, 'With man this is impossible, but with God all things are possible.'"

Personally, I, like the disciples, believe that among all the stages or steps of mankind, Stage Zero is the most difficult to ascend, or break away from. At Stage Zero, as we have learned previously, man is weak because of his deplorable state.

Another major factor lies in the fact that the devil will not allow anyone to leave his domain easily. The devil always puts up a fight against anybody who wants to make a move towards God's way of salvation or break away from him, because the devil wants to have everybody with him in hell, which was originally prepared for him and the fallen angels.

1. But thank God for the Holy Spirit who helps us to make the decision towards God, by believing and accepting Jesus Christ as Lord and Saviour, the only part one has to play. This means that no matter how rich, powerful, intellectual or famous a man may be he is dead in sin, and, therefore, unable alone to progress from Stage Zero: only through faith in Christ, who takes away the sin of the world, is progress possible.

When the disciples asked Jesus to show them the way to the Father, Jesus answered: "I am the way and the truth and the life. No one comes to the Father except through me." (John 14:6)

The work of salvation is totally and exclusively God's, man has only to believe and receive.

As I said earlier, progression through all the stages can be done only through a good healthy diet (the word of God, the Gospel).

Paul said, "I am not ashamed of the Gospel, because it is the power of God for the salvation of everyone who believes: first for the Jew, then for the Gentiles [Greeks]." (Romans 1:16)

This remains true also for people (or mentors) that have ascended from Stage Zero, for only through taking the food – the word of God – will he progress. That is to say that, only by responding to the Gospel about God's plan for salvation, preached by people who can help him move on, would he come alive; without the Gospel, he will remain dead and doomed to hell.

(Romans 10:12–13) "For there is no difference between Jew and Gentile [Greeks] the same Lord of all and richly blesses all who call on him, for, everyone who calls on the name of the Lord will be saved."

(Romans 10:14–15) "How, then, can they call on the one they have not believed in? And how can they believe in the one of whom they have not heard? And how can they hear without someone preaching to them? And how can they preach unless they are sent?

As it is written, 'how beautiful are the feet of those who bring good news!'"

Are you confused, are you wondering what this Stage Zero is all about?

The purpose of Stage Zero is to allow non-believers to get to know the state of life without Christ here on earth. It is also in order to consider the future without Christ. Stage Zero also focuses believers' attention on the state of non-believers, so that they may have passion and pray for them, while also taking the opportunity to present the Gospel of Christ to them and lead them to salvation.

As peter says, the Lord does not want anybody to perish or remain a sinner: "The Lord is not slow in keeping his promises, as some understand slowness. He is patient with you, not wanting anyone to perish but everyone to come to repentance." (2 Peter 3:9)

Knowledge of Stage Zero also helps believers to work out their own salvation with fear and trembling. As you read this book, my advice is this: look again at somebody you know who is not yet born again, and consider him or her in the light of my description of Stage Zero. Have pity on him or her and do your best, first to pray for their salvation and, if possible, present them with the word of God, the Gospel, in the hope that it will bring them to repentance.

A bit about my personal life at Stage Zero

As a young boy, like most people in their teenage years, I was at Stage Zero before I was born again. I was blind and lost; I did not know what I was doing or where I was going. Like many children at Stage Zero, not only was I heading towards hell, but also I made life very difficult and unpleasant for my parents.

During this time, I alone among my mother's children lived with my father, who lived in a different town. One day my father looked straight in my face wearing a very angry expression. He told me that he did not want to be like an animal that abandons its babies, or otherwise he would disown me for the sake of his peace.

Another incident happened when I came back to live with my mother and my other brothers and sisters. One day I went out and had a serious fight with somebody; blood ran from my nose and soaked my shirt, which I regret to confess was a regular occurrence in my early years. My mother, who went into shock and panicked when she saw me covered in blood, said: "I know one day that I will be eating when I receive the news that someone has beaten you to death."

This was the situation: my father wanted to disown me if he could; my mother feared someone may beat me to death one day, and all this was because my life was being controlled by Satan. My Stage Zero attitude caused me to put my parents through a very tough time, which meant that I often offered them a bitter pill to swallow.

Sometimes, just as anyone else at Stage Zero, I was blind and did not know where I was going or what I was doing. Thankfully, God's word and His saving grace rescued me, enabling me to make the great transformation that has brought about such change to my own and others' lives since I received Christ as my Lord and Saviour.

This great change took place on that faithful Sunday in 1975, just as I have already described above. Both my parents witnessed and testified about it. Before my father died in 2009, I believe he had peace and that he loved me as I loved him.

My mother now no longer fears for my life; I never fight now, and my life is controlled by the Spirit of God. What a great transformation Jesus brought about in my life. Many others have been written off, but life in Jesus has transformed their lives also. Jesus will do the same for you if you receive Him into your life. He is a life-changer who transforms life for the better. Praise Him!

To conclude this section about Stage Zero, I would like to bring to the fore the image of life for those stuck at Stage Zero, which is a life so deplorable. By this, I mean that life is hopeless, meaningless, dark without light, they are blind, far away from God, under the power of Satan and dead unto sin. These people cannot help themselves, and they need the Saviour to rescue them from the mess in which they find themselves. What I mean is this: that in order for them to progress to Stage One, their salvation can come about only through the grace of Jesus Christ the Son of God. Without Him, all men remain at Stage Zero and are doomed to hell. There is no alternative. Therefore, if you do not want to be doomed to hell yourself, or if somebody you know is destined for hell, I implore you: do not stop reading this book; I urge you to read on.

Stage One: the Repentance Stage

Stage One is the first step of man's transformation; the journey to salvation and life after. It is when a person has responded to the Gospel or the good news, recognises himself as a sinner, and therefore repents and is regenerated; that is, when he or she is born again. This is the beginning of man's journey to heaven; the future home for believers, it is the day when one says "Yes" to the call of God and receives Jesus Christ into his life. This is the moment when man reconnects with God as his creator and, therefore, decides to live for Him and serve Him.

In life, one must make many decisions; to get married, start a family, study or maybe change the course of our study, change the job we do or the friends we keep. We may decide to travel at some point in our lives, and so on, but I believe that to make the decision to progress from Stage Zero to Stage One is the best decision any man can ever make in his entire life. Turning away from Stage Zero – the Sinful Stage – to move to Stage One – the Repenting Stage – is to turn around and view and experience everything differently. To move from Stage Zero to Stage One is to move from hell to heaven, from darkness to light, from a meaningless life to a meaningful life; from a life without hope to one full of hope, from an existence under the power of Satan to life under the power of God through Christ, from eternal death to eternal life, and many, many more benefits.

Why do we need Stage One to be born again? Or why is man's second birth so important?

Man's rebirth is important, for without it no one will inherit the kingdom of God, which is to remain without being born again, and man will be doomed to hell for eternity. No one can inherit the kingdom of God with his sinful nature intact at Stage Zero. Even the old man needs to be born again. Furthermore, man needed a saviour to save him and reconcile or reconnect him to God, since a life without Christ means a broken relationship with God.

As the name Jesus denotes, He came to earth to save mankind (Matthew 1:21), because we cannot save ourselves from sin and its circumstances. No matter how good we are, no one can eliminate his own sinful nature. Only Jesus has been given the mandate to do that. On His mission, Jesus came, not to help people to save themselves, but He came to save man from the power and penalty of sin. As you read this book, I once again advise you to submit to His power and allow Him to save you and take control of your life. Talking to Nicodemus Jesus said to him, "I tell you the truth, no-one can see the kingdom of God unless he is born again." And Jesus reiterated this message by saying, "I tell you the truth, no-one can enter the kingdom of God unless he is born of water and the spirit." (John 3:3–5)

Like a moth or a butterfly trapped within an enclosed space without any hope of escape, so man is equally trapped without Christ. Man is helpless. Because it is not easy for man to save himself, it takes God to work out man's plan for salvation. To assist us, God provides His own Son; He alone is worthy to save man from his sinful, deplorable state. The Bible says that, through Adam, sin was imputed to all men, and through Christ, righteousness was also imputed to all who believe. Paul in a series of Bible quotations affirms this:

"Yet he did not waver through unbelief regarding the promise of God, but was strengthened in his faith and gave glory to God, being fully persuaded that God had power to do what He had promised. This is why 'it was credited to him as righteousness.' The words 'it was credited to him' were not written for Him alone, but also for us, to whom God will credit righteousness – for us who believe in Him who raised Jesus our Lord from the dead. He was delivered over to death for our sins and was raised to life for our justification." (Romans 4:20–25)

"For as in Adam all die, so in Christ all will make alive." (1 Corinthians 15:22)

"Therefore, if anyone is in Christ, he is a new creation; the old has gone, the new has come! All this is from God, who reconciled us to Himself through Christ and gave us the ministry of reconciliation: that God was reconciling the world to Himself in Christ, not counting men's sins against them. And he has committed to us the message of reconciliation. We are therefore Christ's ambassadors, as though God were making his appeal through us. We implore you on Christ's behalf: Be reconciled to God. God made Him who had no sin to be sin for us, so that in him we might become the righteousness of God." (2 Corinthians 5:17–21)

Like a man trapped deep down inside a hole, God our caring Father, will lower Christ down to us like a rope; He will throw down the lifeline to all who seek Him; He saves all those who seek Him; He saves all those who take hold of the rope so that the Father can bring them up to safety. Christ is the saviour of mankind. If you are one of those, like a butterfly trapped within an enclosed space, or a man imprisoned deep down inside a hole; if you are a non-believer reading this book, then I advise you to 'be transformed', that is, set your foot on the road to spiritual transformation; think of yourself in this state of horror while God lowers Christ down to you, ready to lift you out of your hole and set you free from the danger, without any charge.

God revealed His plan for man's salvation before He had created man

Contrary to the views of those who believe that God created the universe but then did not care what happened to it, that is, God has set the universe in motion but does not interfere with how it runs (**Deism**) I want to say as I have said repeatedly, God does care for mankind. Knowing that man could not save himself from his deplorable state, He revealed His great plan to redeem the world through Christ. On the very day that Adam and Eve sinned. He said:

"And I will put enmity between you and the woman, and between your offspring and hers; he will crush your head, and you will strike his heel." (Genesis 3:15)

When referring to this, God's wonderful and perfect plan for man's salvation, Paul said:

(Ephesians 1:3) "Praise be to the God and Father of our Lord Jesus Christ, who was blessed us in the heavenly realms with every spiritual blessing in Christ."

(Ephesians 1:4) "For he chose us in him before the creation of the world to be holy and blameless in his sight."

(Ephesians 1:5) "In love he persuaded us to be adopted as his sons through Jesus Christ, in accordance with his pleasure and will."

(2 Timothy 1:9–10) "…who has saved us and called us to a holy life – not because of anything we have done but because of his own purpose and grace. This grace was given us in Christ Jesus before the beginning of time, but it has now been revealed through the appearing of our saviour Christ Jesus, who has destroyed death and has brought life and immortality to light through the Gospel."

In addition, in Titus (1:2), Paul said "… a faith and knowledge resting on the hope of eternal life, which God, who does not lie, promised before the beginning of time …"

Again, in Matthew (1:21), the Angel of the Lord tells Joseph "She will give birth to a son, and you are to give him the name Jesus, because he will save his people from their sins."

(Galatians 4:4–5) "But when the time had fully come, God sent his Son, born of a woman, born under law, to redeem those under law, that we might receive the full rights of sons."

(2 Peter 3:9) "The Lord is not slow in keeping his promise, as some understand slowness. He is patient with you, not wanting anyone to perish but everyone to come to repentance."

It is through Jesus and only through Him that man can progress from Stage Zero to Stage One. That is to say,

Jesus is the only bridge or ladder over which man can walk and progress, taking one step in front of another.

On this note, may I remind you with all due respect to other religions outside Christianity that my advice and call to you is this: if you want eternal life, an everlasting life, a life that never ends, then there is only one Man, the seed of the woman (Genesis 3:15), and that Man is Jesus, as the only begotten Son of God. (Galatians 4:4–5)

"I am the way and the truth and the life" (John 14:6). On his instructions of worship to Timothy, Paul said, "For there is one God and one mediator between God and Men, the man Christ Jesus, who gave himself as a ransom for all men the testimony given in its proper time." (1Timothy 2:5–6)

Salvation is for everyone

According to Paul, God has not chosen anybody to go to hell, but wants everyone to receive salvation: "For God did not appoint us to suffer wrath but to receive salvation through our Lord Jesus Christ. He dies for us so that, whether we are awake or asleep, we may live together with Him. Therefore encourage one another and build each other up, just as in fact you are doing." (1 Thessalonians 5:9–11)

"This is good, and pleases God our Saviour, who wants all men to be saved and to come to knowledge of the truth." (1 Timothy 2:3–4)

Instructing Titus what to teach various groups in the church, He said, "For the grace of God that brings salvation has appeared to all men." (Titus 2:11)

Remember what Peter said: "The Lord is not slow in keeping his promise, as some understand slowness. He is patient with you, not wanting anyone to perish, but everyone come to repentance." (2 Peter 3:9)

Although man sins greatly by disobeying God, He still loves mankind and does not want anybody to perish. He gave His only begotten Son so that man could be saved through Him.

Luke records that on the night of Jesus' birth, an angel tried to reassure the shepherds who were taking care of their sheep in the fields that night. They were terrified of the light that shone all around them, in the presence of the angel, in the glory of God. The angel said, "Do not be afraid. I bring you good news of great joy that will be for all the people. Today in the town of David a Saviour has been born to you; he is Christ the Lord." (Luke 2:10–11)

The salvation of God; Jesus Christ has come for all people.

On reflection

(John 3:16) "For ***God*** so ***loved*** the ***world*** that he gave his only begotten son that ***whosoever*** believes in Him shall not perish but have eternal life."

The quotation above dates back to the religious leader, Nicodemus, who went to Jesus by night seeking the truth from Him. In telling him the truth (John 3:16), Jesus said, "For God so loved …". Therefore, as we discuss "salvation for all", before we continue any further; let us first reflect on the four key words in this verse:

I am happy to take a few minutes with you to explain the four key words in John (3:16) because to me they are very important so far as the salvation of mankind is connected to them:

1. God
2. Love
3. The World
4. Whoever

God

I believe that it is not difficult to explain who God is, even though some people believe that there is no God. For the majority of people, however, although they may not yet have given their lives to Him, they believe there is a supreme being somewhere who created the world and all that is upon it. To answer the question "who is God?" I will say quite simply to you, just as Jesus said to the Samaritan woman, "God is spirit, and his worshippers must worship in spirit and in truth." (John 4:24)

In the Old Testament, we see that God revealed Himself to the children of Israel by His Names, Acts and Attributes. In the New Testament, Paul, in a letter to the Romans, writes to all those people who hold the same view as those who argue about the fate of people, living before the birth of Christ. He says that no one has any excuse for not knowing God, for God has revealed Himself through creation, saying:

"The wrath of God is being revealed from heaven against all the godlessness and wickedness of men who suppress the truth by their wickedness, since what may be known about God is plain to them. For since the creation of the world God's visible qualities, his eternal power and divine nature have been clearly seen, being understood from what has been made, so that men are without excuse." (Romans 1:18–20)

In the Psalm (19:1–3) David says: "The heavens declare the glory of God; the skies proclaim the work of his hands. Day after Day they pour forth speech; night after night they display knowledge. There is no speech or language where their voice is not heard." What this means is, even though there are many people and languages on the face of the earth, none of these can claim not to have heard the voice of God, because He is the God of all flesh. The fact that God exists cannot be denied by anybody, for it is clear and obvious everywhere that there is a God.

Love

Unlike in the English language, in Greek, there are *four* words for love:

We have **Eros**, who represents the physical, carnal, passionate and erotic; love of the flesh; passionate feelings of romantic desire and sexual attraction.

Then there is **Philia**, the love between friends. Friendship is the strong bond existing between people who share common interests or activities.

Another one **Storge**, which is fondness through familiarity; that is, a brotherly or family love, especially between family members such as parents and children and brothers and sisters

Then, finally, there is that of **Agape**, the love of God. This is an unconditional love. In His love, God set up the pattern of true love, the basis of all relationships and the love of self-sacrifice. God demonstrated His love by sacrificing the life of His only dear Son.

Sacrificial love is the love that God gave, not the love man wanted or deserved but one that God perceived man needed. By giving man Jesus Christ, His only precious Son, He gave forgiveness to mankind. God is the only One that gives this unselfish kind of love, the *Agape* love.

Agape love is the love that brings forth caring, regardless of the circumstance. This is the greatest of all the loves.

The world

I have studied the notion of "the world" in the Scriptures, where there are three different definitions. I am happy to discuss all of them so that believers may know which one of them we are dealing with in the context of John (3:16).

1. The universe or the earth

All allusions to "the world" in the quotations below refer to the universe, the cosmos and the earth.

"Again, the devil took him to a very high mountain and showed him all the kingdoms of the world and their splendour." (Matthew 4:8)

"Jesus did many other things as well. If every one of them were written down, I suppose that even the whole world would not have room for the books that would be written." (John 21:25)

"If I were hungry I would not tell you, for the world is mine, and all that is in it." (Psalm 50:12)

2. Material things and the pleasures of the world

"And how do you benefit if you gain the whole world but lose your own soul in the process? Is anything worth more than your soul?" (Matthew 16:26)

"Next the devil took him to the peak of a very high mountain and showed him the nations of the world and all their glory. I will give it all to you, he said, 'If you will only kneel down and worship me.'" (Matthew 4:8–9)

"Yet they cannot redeem themselves from death by paying a ransom to God. Redemption does not come so easily, for no one can ever pay enough to live forever and never see the grave. Those who are wise must finally die, just like the foolish and senseless, leaving all their wealth behind. The grave is their eternal home, where they will stay forever. They may name their estates after themselves, but they leave their wealth to others. They will not last long, despite their riches; they will die like the animals." (Psalm 49:7–12)

"Do not love the world or anything in the world. If anyone loves the world, the love of the Father is not in him. For everything in the world the cravings of sinful man, the lust of his eyes and the boasting of what he has and does comes not from the Father but from the world. The world and its desires pass away, but the man who does the will of God lives for ever." (1 John 2:15–17)

I believe that one of the devil's greatest enticements is to lure Christians through their lust for material wealth. Therefore, Christians must be very careful how they chase material things. Through lust for material things, the devil can easily lure you into his kingdom, just as he tried to do to Jesus. Another interesting factor of this is that, if the devil tried to entice Jesus Christ by offering Him the material things of the world, things that you could say belong to Him anyway, imagine how he would pressure you, who may not even know that if you first seek the kingdom of God and His righteousness, all these things will be gifted to you anyway.

3. The people or inhabitants of the world
"He was in the world, and though the world was made through him, the world did not recognise him." (1 John 1:10)

This quotation speaks of both the earth and the people or the inhabitants of the world.

(John 3:16) "For God so loved the world, that he gave his one and only son, that whoever believes in him shall not perish but have eternal life."

(Mark 16:15) "He said to them, 'Go into all the world and preach the good news to all creation.'"

(1 John 2:2) "He is the atoning sacrifice for our sins, and not only for ours but also for the sins of the whole world."

(2 Corinthians 5:18) "All this is from God, who reconciled us to himself through Christ, and give us the mystery of reconciliation …"

(2 Corinthians 5:19) "… that God was reconciling the world to himself in Christ, not counting men's sins against them. And he has committed to us the message of reconciliation."

(2 Corinthians 5:20) "We are therefore Christ's ambassadors, as though God were making his appeal through us. We implore you on Christ's behalf: Be reconciled to God."

(2 Corinthians 5:21) "God made him who had no sin to be sin for us, so that in him we might become the righteousness of God."

This notion of belief is more than just believing that Jesus is God, as James said:

"You believe that there is one God. Good! Even the demons believe that and shudder!" (James 2:19)

Belief means that we must put our trust and confidence wholly in God, for only He can save us. Put your trust in Christ, put Him in charge of all that we do: believe and trust in Him that His words are reliable and rely on Him for the power that can change the course of your life. If you have not yet trusted or given your life to Him, let this promise of eternal life be yours, and believe. No one is guaranteed to receive salvation except those who believe in Christ. Jesus said, "I am the way and the truth and the life. No one comes to the Father except through me." (John 14:6)

How to be born again

The steps to salvation: the first step of spiritual transformation may seem elementary to many, especially those who have already been born again. I, on the other hand, see the steps to salvation as one of the greatest subjects in Christianity.

Through the grace of God I received Christ and was born again that faithful Sunday in 1975, just as I related earlier in my personal story. God will not call others in the same way; He will call us all by different means. From the steps I set out below, believers will learn how to witness to non-believers as we respond to Jesus' Great Commission.

"Therefore go and make disciples of all the nations, baptising them in the name of the Father and of the Son and of the Holy Spirit, and teaching them to obey everything I have commanded you. And surely I am with you always, to the very end of the age." Amen. (Matthew 28:19–20)

If you are reading this book as a non-believer, you can also follow these steps to receive Christ as Lord and Saviour.

1. Everyone intending to progress from Stage Zero must first know, believe and accept that, without Christ, s/he is a sinner. This is very important, for it is not until one recognises this, that genuine repentance is possible.
2. Know that you became a sinner through Adam and Eve (all men are sinners at Stage Zero).
3. Recognise that the wages of sins committed is death.
4. Know that death is separation from God (everyone at Stage Zero is dead and separated from God).
5. Man needs a saviour for he cannot save himself. It is only through Jesus that anyone can be saved. Jesus is the only mediator between God and man. "This is good, and pleases God our Saviour, who wants all men to be saved and to come to knowledge of the truth. For there is one God and one mediator between God and men, the man Christ Jesus, who gave himself as a ransom for all men – the testimony given in its proper time." (1 Timothy 2:3–6)

6. That God sent Jesus to die for us, to save all those who will believe His name and bring them back to him. (Matthew 1:21; Romans 5:8, 5:18; Hebrews 9:26; 1 Peter 2:24)

7. To repent and forsake sin. (Proverbs 28, 13; Matthew 3:2, 4:17; Mark 1:15; 1 John 1:9)

8. Invite or receive Christ into your heart as Lord and Saviour. (John 3:35–36; 6:37; Acts 4:10–12; Romans 10:9–10)

"That if you confess with your mouth, 'Jesus is Lord,' and believe in your heart that God has raised him from the dead, you will be saved. For it is with your heart that you believe and are justified, and it is with your mouth that you confess and are saved." (Romans 10:9–10)

Salvation is for all, but salvation is personal

Salvation comes only through Jesus; He is the only mediator between God and man. Although salvation is for everybody, it is also personal; that is, it is not tied to nationality or ethnicity; is not dependent on whether your parents are believers. Salvation is achieved through a personal relationship with Jesus Christ, through your own faith in Christ. What this means is that you are not born again because you are a Jew, a descendant of Abraham, or because your parents are born again. My children as I speak now are not automatically born again because I am a Pastor; they are born again because they have received Christ as their personal Lord and Saviour.

Years ago, there was a man who was my presiding Elder. One Sunday morning he brought all his grown-up children to church and made an announcement directed at them before the whole church. I will quote exactly what he said: "Even though you are my children you are not born again because I am your father. You will be born again only when each of you, one by one, personally receive Christ into your heart." His children then praised God in front of the whole congregation; one after the other they received Christ and confessed Him as Lord and Saviour.

The Apostle John said, "He came to that which was his own, but his own did not receive him. Yet to all who receive him, to those who believed in his name, he gave the right to become children of God – children born not of natural descent, nor of human decision or a husband's will, but born of God." (John 1:11–13)

(John 3:36) "Whoever believes in the Son has eternal life, but whoever rejects the Son will not see life, for God's wrath remains on him."

(Romans 5:16) "Again the gift of God is not like result of the one man's sin: The judgement followed one sin and brought condemnation, but the gift followed many trespasses and brought justification."

Another important point to note is the fact that, unlike the manner in which all men became sinners through the sins of Adam and Eve, you do not become born again through your parents, but by repentance through faith in Jesus Christ. Therefore, if your parents are Christians and you think you are automatically born again because of them, please change your thinking or renew your mind, for salvation is brought about by your personal relationship with God through faith in Christ Jesus. I know of so many people who were born of Christian parents and have therefore been in the church since they were born, but are not yet born again. You may ask me how I knew they were not born again. My answer is this: by their fruit you will know them; Christ is not only our saviour but also our Lord.

Another point is this: just as being physically born places you in your parents' family, so also it is true that to be born again of God places you spiritually within God's family. That is, to progress from Stage Zero to Stage One, all those who welcome Jesus Christ into their hearts by believing in His name, are born again, spiritually transformed.

Let me repeat this in order to reassure you that spiritual transformation is not brought about because you are a Jew, or because you have been going to church for long time, or because you were born into a Christian home. It is brought about through your own personal faith in

Christ. No one is good enough to save him or herself. Apart from Christ, there is no other way for our sins to be forgiven and removed. John says that you are not a child of God because you are Jewish or because of the family from which you came; you become the son of God only when you are born of the Spirit, and to do that, you must believe in the name of Jesus Christ under the influence of the Holy Spirit.

Salvation through grace

Salvation is attainable purely by grace (underserved mercy) and no one can attain salvation through good works alone. To get to stand beside God can never be attained through good woks or through our actions; it is only attainable through the standard set by God. No one can match this standard through deeds except through God's grace (undeserved mercy). God does not measure our standard of righteousness through our works, but by our relationship with His Son who alone is qualified to bring salvation to mankind.

I remember being at a meeting once where the preacher was teaching about salvation through grace, attained through faith in Jesus Christ. He invited the congregation to ask him some questions. One man asked passionately the following question: "I have many friends who are not Christians but they are very good people, so Mr. preacher, are you saying that, despite all the good things done by these friends, they cannot go to heaven because they are not Christians or without Christ?"

"Yes," replied the preacher, "for no one goes to heaven because he is good; Christ is the only way to heaven." Paul writing to the church in Ephesus said, "For it is by grace you have been saved and this is not from yourselves, it is the gift of God – not by works so that no one can boast." (Ephesians 2:8–9)

The Bible says that during the time of Moses, God choose the people of Israel out of all the other people on the earth; not because of any work they did for Him, but in keeping His promise to their ancestors. In the same way, He has also chosen all believers, not because of their individual efforts, but by grace through faith in Christ.

Moses told the children of Israel: "The Lord did not set his affection on you and choose you because you were more numerous than other people, for you were the fewest of all people. But it was because the Lord loved you and kept the oath he swore to your fore fathers that he brought you out with a mighty hand and redeemed you from the land of slavery, from the power of Pharaoh King of Egypt. Know therefore that the Lord your God is God; He is the faithful God, keeping his covenant of Love to a thousand generations of those who love him and keep his commands." (Deuteronomy 7:7–9)

Again, Moses says to the people of Israel that it is not because of their righteousness that the Lord gave them the Promised Land, but because of the wickedness of those living in the land. He also said that he was keeping his promise to their forefathers.

"After the Lord your God has driven them before you, do not say to yourself, 'The Lord has brought me here to take possession of this land because of my righteousness.' No, it is because of the wickedness of these nations that the Lord is going to drive them out before you. It is not because of your righteousness or your integrity that you are going to take possession of the land; but on account of the wickedness of these nations, the Lord your God will drive them out before you, to accomplish what he swore to your fathers, to Abraham, Isaac and Jacob. Understand, then, that it is not because of your righteousness that the Lord your God is giving you this good land to possess, for you are a stiff-necked people." (Deuteronomy 9:4–6)

Isaiah said (64:6) "All of us have become like one who is unclean, and all our righteous acts are like filthy rags; we all shrivel up like a leaf, and like the win our sins sweep us away."

This means that even when we are trying our best to be good, the result is like filthy rags before God. We can only do good things through Him, for as He said, "I am the vine; you are the branches. If a man remains in me and I in him, he will bear much fruit; apart from me you can do nothing." (John 15:5)

Paul reaffirms this in the following scripture: "Therefore no one will be declared righteous in his sight by observing the law; rather through the law we become conscious of sin." (Romans 3:20)

There are many instances in the Bible to remind us that faith is paramount to salvation:

(Romans 11:6) "And if by grace, then it is no longer of works; if it were, grace would be no longer grace."

(Galatians 2:16) "Know that a man is not justified by observing the law, but by faith in Jesus Christ. So we, too, have put our faith in Christ Jesus that we may be justified by faith in Christ and not by observing the law, because by observing the law no-one will be justified."

(Ephesians 2:8–9) "For it is by grace you have been saved, through faith – and this not from yourselves, it is the gift of God – not by works, so that no-one can boast."

(2 Timothy 1:9) "Who has saved us and called us to a holy life – not because of anything we have done but because of his own purpose and grace. This grace was given us in Christ Jesus before the beginning of time."

Assurance of salvation

Being certain of your salvation is as important as being born again. When you are not sure of what you have, you can easily loose it, so it is better to be certain in the knowledge that you are saved. There are those that, because they are not sure of their salvation, and in their ignorance, at every meeting or service, they respond to altar call. Others use altar-call to go forward so that they will be prayed for on other issues. Receiving Christ into my heart, being born again, happened for me just once, not repeatedly.

Witnessing to a woman some time ago, I asked her if she was sure of her salvation, whether she was sure that she would go to heaven to be with Christ when she died. To my surprise, she answered me angrily saying, "How can I be sure, for no one knows if he or she will go to heaven when they die." She was obviously unsure of her salvation, even though she had been a Christian for many years. If you, like this woman, are struggling and not sure whether you are born again and will go to heaven to be with Christ when you die, then here are some Scriptures that will help you to know whether you are truly saved or not.

(1 John 1:11–13) "He came to that which was his own, but his own did not receive him. Yet to all who received him, to those who believed in his name, he gave them the right to become children of God – children

born not of natural descent, nor of human decision or a husband's will, but born of God."

(Galatians 3:26–29) "You are all sons of God through faith in Christ Jesus for all of you who were baptised into Christ have clothed yourselves with Christ. There is neither Jew nor Greek, slave nor free, male nor female, for you are all one in Christ Jesus. If you belong to Christ, then you are Abraham's seed, and heirs according to the promise."

(Romans 9:6–9) "It is not as though God's word had failed. For not all who are descended from Israel is Israel. Nor because they are his descendants are they all Abraham's children. On the contrary, it is through Isaac that your offspring will be reckoned." Please note that the natural children are not considered to be God's children but the children of the promise, who are regarded as Abraham's offspring. For this was how the promise was stated: "At the appointed time I will return, and Sarah will have a son."

(Genesis 21:12–13) "But God said to him [Abraham], 'Do not be so distressed about the boy and your maidservant. Listen to whatever Sarah tells you, because it is through Isaac that your offspring will be reckoned. I will make the son of the maidservant into a nation also, because he is your offspring.'"

(Galatians 3:16) "The promises were spoken to Abraham and his seed. The Scripture does not say 'and to seeds', meaning many people, but 'and to your seed', meaning one person, who is Christ."

(1 John 5:12–13) "He who has the Son has life; he who does not have the son of God does not have life. I write these things to you who believe in the name of the Son of God so that you may know that you have eternal life.

(Genesis 22:18) "… and through your offspring all nations on earth will be blessed, because you have obeyed me."

To sum up everything we have considered here, I would like to tell all of you who are not sure of your salvation, and who, therefore, are unable to answer this simple question: "Are you saved or born again?" I want you to know that salvation comes through your faith in Jesus Christ.

If on the other hand, you know that you have truly received Christ as LORD and saviour and that you are, therefore, living for Him, then know that, and get it truly settled in your heart.

Know in your heart that you are saved or have been born again. Know also that you will either go to heaven when you die or you will be in rapture with Him when He appears at His second coming to His home.

Another point I believe will be useful to you is this: when you are sure of your salvation, when you know that you have been saved by Jesus, it helps if you live for Him and then submit to His will.

The result of being born again: A new creation!

Being born again brings so many benefits to mankind. Some of these benefits I have detailed below. One result of being born again, according to Paul, is that you are a new creation:

"Therefore, if anyone is in Christ, he is a new creation; the old has gone; the new has come!" (2 Corinthians 5:17)

As Paul says, in order to become new, the old things must pass away. This means that all the things related to the old person have gone. We are adopted into a new family, God's family: "Yet to all who received him, to those who believed in his name, he gave the right to become children of God – children born not of natural descent, nor of human decision or a husband's will, but born of God." (John 1:12–13)

"For you did not receive a spirit that makes you a slave again to fear, but you received the Spirit of sonship [adoption]. And by him we cry, 'Abba, Father.'" (Romans 8:15)

(Galatians 4:4–5) "But when the time had fully come, God sent his son, born of a woman, born under the law, to redeem those under law, that we might receive the full rights of sins."

(Ephesians 1:5) "... he predestined us to be adopted as his sons through Jesus Christ, in accordance with his pleasure and will ..."

Paul mentions adoption several times in his letters, because during Paul's time – just as it is now – it was part of Roman culture to adopt children.

To reiterate, all believers are adopted into God's family when they are born again. In order to gain more understanding of the notion of adoption, it is worth considering the word and all its meanings:

- Someone who takes a child into his own family and treats him or her as his own child.
- Someone received as a son or daughter into a family even though she or he was not so born.
- Giving to someone the name, place and privileges of a son or daughter, although not a son or daughter by birth.

As I mentioned earlier, in Roman culture during Paul's time, the adopted child lost all the rights and privileges of his old family and gained all the rights and privileges as a legitimate child within his new family. He became a rightful heir to his adopted father's and mother's assets. Similarly, when someone becomes a Christian or is born again, he gains all the rights and loosens all bondage, curses or any other demonic influences that belong with his or her former family, and to gain instead a life full of blessings within his or her new family – God's family.

As recorded in the Scriptures, Moses enjoyed all the privileges of an Egyptian when he was adopted as Pharaoh's daughter son:

(Hebrews 11:24) "By faith, Moses, when he had grown up, refused to be known as the son of Pharaoh's daughter."

(Hebrews 11:25) "He chose to be ill-rated along with the people of God rather than to enjoy the pleasures of sin for a short time."

(Hebrews 11:26) "He regarded disgrace for the sake of Christ as of greater value than the treasures of Egypt, because he was looking ahead to his reward."

With adoption in mind, the big question is why do some born-again Christians, who have supposedly been adopted into God's family, still suffer from the curses and bondages of their old family ties so that they are unable to enjoy the freedom of their new family? The answer is simple; it is due to ignorance, for it is said (Hosea 4:6), "My people are destroyed from lack of knowledge."

Without a doubt, another reason for this continuing situation lies in those who profess to hold to the Christian faith, but who, in fact, are not practising Christians.

Believers that lack knowledge of who they are in Christ can be likened to a chicken that has been covered with a basket for a long time. When later the basket is taken away, the chicken still does not move, because it believes it is still beneath the basket. It also brings to mind the sheep that jumps a rope out of necessity to get to a particular place, and even when the rope has been removed, the sheep continues to jump over the rope.

Reconciled to God

The theme of reconciliation and reconnection runs throughout the Scriptures.

At Stage Zero, we noted that man without Christ has lost connection with God because of sin. A man who has lost the glory of God, who has lost all that God intended for him can, thank God, through faith in Jesus, become a believer and be reconciled or reconnected with God; he can return to God and regain sonship and the lost Glory of God, as Paul said: "For all have sinned and fallen short of the glory of God, and are justified freely by his grace through the redemption that came by Christ Jesus." (Romans 3:23–24)

Also in (Romans 5:10) Paul said, "For if, then, we were God's enemies, we were reconciled to him through the death of his son, how much more, having been reconciled, shall we be saved through his life!"

(Romans 5:11) "Not only is this so, through the disobedience of the one man the many were made sinners, so also through the obedience of the one man the many will be made righteous."

(Colossians 1:21) "Once you were alienated from God and were enemies in your minds because of your evil behaviour."

(Colossians 1:22) "But now he has reconciled you by Christ's physical body through death to present you holy in his sight, without blemish and free from accusation."

(Ephesians 2:11) "Therefore, remember that formerly you who are Gentiles by birth and called 'uncircumcised' by those who call themselves 'the circumcision' (that done to the body by the hands of men) …"

(Ephesians 2:12) "… remember that at that time you were separated from Christ, excluded from citizenship in Israel and foreigners to the covenants of the promise, without hope and without God in the world."

(Ephesians 2:13) "But now in Christ Jesus you who once were far away have been brought near through the blood of Christ."

(Ephesians 2:19) "Consequently, you are no longer foreigners and aliens, but fellow-citizens with God's people and members of God's household."

(Ephesians 2:20) "… built on the foundation of the apostles and prophets, with Christ Jesus himself as the chief cornerstone."

(Ephesians 2:21) "In him the whole building is joined together and rises to become a holy temple in the LORD."

(Ephesians 2:22) "And in him you too are being built together to become a dwelling in which God lives by his Spirit."

God becomes our Father

Through faith in Christ, Christians become sons and daughters of God and can go to Him at any time for anything, just as a child approaches his father (physically) any time he is in need, without any fear or panic. When I was a child, I would go to my parents' bedroom at any time without knocking, just as my children do now, entering the comfort and safety of the parents' bedroom when at any time they feel the need to do so.

Faith in God through Jesus Christ gives Christians free access to God as His children.

These Scriptures attest to the notion that through faith in God we are His children:

(John 1:12) "Yet to all who received him, to those who believed in his name, he gave the right to become children of God."

(John 1:13) "Children born not of natural descent, nor of human decision, or a husband's will, but born of God."

(2 Corinthians 6:18) "'I will be a Father to you, and you will be my sons and daughters', says the LORD Almighty."

When Jesus was asked by His disciples to teach them prayers, He said: "This, then, is how you should pray: 'Our Father in heaven, hallowed is your name ...'" (Matthew 6:9)

And again, when teaching them how to be persistent in prayer, He said, "If you then, though you are evil, know how to give good gifts to your children, how much more will your Father in heaven give the Holy Spirit to those who ask him." (Luke 11:13)

Let it be taken as great encouragement for all believers who have been reconciled to God, that when God becomes your Father, it takes just a little courage, while giving enormous joy to approach God for anything we need at any time without any hesitation.

For example, my nephew lived with us when my sister went away for a time, and I noticed that on many occasions my nephew found it very difficult to approach me when he was in need of something, whereas my daughter would approach me at any time to ask for something she needed, even coming to my bedroom without knocking. However, the good news is that Jesus said God our heavenly Father cares for us even more than our earthly fathers do. For this reason, the writer of Hebrews said, "Let us then approach the throne of grace with confidence, so that we may receive mercy and find grace to help us in our time of need." (Hebrews 4:16)

"This is the confidence we have in approaching God: that is we ask anything according to his will, he hears us ..." (1 John 5:14)

Believers Pass from Darkness to Light
(John 1:4) "In him was life, and the life was the light of men."

(John 1:5) "The light shines in the darkness, but the darkness was not understood."

Then Jesus spoke to them again, saying:

(John 8:12) "I am the light of the world. Whoever follows me will never walk in darkness, but will have the light of life."

(John 12:46) "I have come into the world as light, so that no-one who believes in me should stay in darkness."

Jesus Christ is the light that came into the world. The Bible says that all those who believe in Him have passed from darkness to light. Similarly, it comes as a great relief for a person locked up in a dark room for a long time when the lights are turned on; or imagine a village that has never had access to electricity and the joy of the inhabitants on that first night when the lights are turned on. This is the mood of the believer when Christ, the light of the world, is "turned on" and comes into their life, at which point the darkness disappears.

This is the reason that believers are always in the spotlight and are always criticised, because we cannot hide. On the other hand, non-believers are hardly seen and criticised, because they are in darkness. May I remind you all, therefore, my fellow believers, to be extra careful about all that you do; knowing that you have passed from darkness to light, so it is that you are in the spotlight, and can easily be seen by all.

(1 Thessalonians 5:4) "But you brothers are not in darkness so that this day should surprise you like a thief."

(1 Thessalonians 5:5) "You are all sons of the light and sons of the day. We do not belong to the night or to the darkness."

(1 Thessalonians 5:6) "So then, let us not be like others, who are asleep, but let us be alert and self-controlled."

Just as the Apostle Paul advises the Thessalonians' Church, let me do the same here and say to all believers: exercise self-control at all times; know that we cannot go to all places and cannot do all the things, although many people may be going there, or doing that. There is a proverb in *Twi* (a Ghanaian language) that says, "Many animals eat the palm nuts, but the squirrel only is always accused." Similarly, all animals will run, but when a cow runs, it is thought to have gone mad.

What I mean is this: yes, everybody may do as they please, but Christians will be accused for doing exactly as they please. Non-believers know that they can do whatever they choose, but this is not so for believers, because it is not right for them to act in such a way.

For this reason, writing to the church in Corinth (1 Corinthians 6:12 and 1 Corinthians 10:23 respectively), Paul said:

"'I have the right to do anything,' you say—but not everything is beneficial. 'I have the right to do anything'—but I will not be mastered by anything.

'I have the right to do anything,' you say—but not everything is beneficial. 'I have the right to do anything'—but not everything is constructive."

This is what I call the limitations of Christian liberty.

Believers pass from death to life
Man died spiritually in the Garden of Eden, disconnected from God. But faith in Christ restores life.

(John 5:24) "I tell you the truth; whoever hears my word and believes him who sent me has eternal life and will not be condemned; he has crossed over from death to life."

(John 3:14–15) "Just as Moses lifted up the snake in the desert, so the Son of man must be lifted, that everyone who believes in him may have eternal life."

(1 John 5:13) "I write these things to you who believe in the name of the Son of God so that you may know that you have eternal life."

Believers receive God's blessing
God promised to bless the whole world through Abraham: that is through his seed, the seed is Jesus Christ.

Therefore, all those who believe in Jesus Christ are blessed as children of Abraham.

(Galatians 3:29) "If you belong to Christ, then you are Abraham's seeds, and heirs according to the promise." This is the promise that was made to Abraham.

(Genesis 12:2) "I will make you into a great nation and I will bless you; I will make your name great, and you will be a blessing."

(Genesis 12:3) "I will bless those who bless you, and whoever curses you I will curse; and all peoples on earth will be blessed through you."

I remember some years ago the title of a book written by a former Pastor: *Abraham's Blessings Are Mine*. In it, the Pastor advised all believers to know and, therefore, claim their rightful portion of the blessing of Abraham, since their faith in Christ gives them that right. I too believe that this valuable treasure every believer should discover: know that you share Abraham's blessing. The lives of many believers would change for the better if they knew and believed that they too were blessed exactly like the Jewish people who are the descendants of Abraham.

Live a Christ-like Life

As we have been promised the same blessing made to Abraham, through faith in Jesus Christ we must walk and live on this earth, as Christ did – a holy and separated life. If it is the case, that we have the blessing of Christ, then believers must lead a Christ-like life. You cannot claim to be a Christian while still leading a life immersed in the chattels of the world.

Teaching on the assurance of salvation at one of our Bible study sessions, again, someone asked me a very important question: "Pastor, won't people take advantage of the fact that salvation only comes from, can only be guaranteed through faith in Jesus Christ, and then lead an unworthy life? Won't people take salvation for granted?"

My answer to this is simple: I believe we receive Christ not only as a saviour, as many know, but also as LORD. Therefore, we must live according to His ways and not ours. We are supposed to lead a Christ-life life; our life must reflect that we are followers of Christ. Luke relates to us in the Book of Acts that the disciples were first called Christians in Antioch because they reflected on Christ: "… and when he had found him, he brought him to Antioch. So for a whole year Barnabas and Saul met the church and taught great numbers of people. The disciples were called Christians first at Antioch." (Acts 11:26)

A line from a song goes, "If you have seen Jesus let his works follow you too". This, I feel is very apt when reflecting on the Lord through all that you do. Remember that your actions should reflect your faith. Morally, you should live above reproach, so that you will reflect God's goodness to others. Jesus made this very plain when He was talking to His disciples and all believers in His Sermon on the Mount.

He said (Matthew 5:13) "You are the salt of the earth. But if the salt loses its saltiness, how can it be made salty again? It is no longer good for anything. Except to be thrown out and trampled by men."

(Matthew 5:14) "You are the light of the world. A city on a hill cannot be hidden."

(Matthew 5:15) "Neither do people light a lamp and put it under a bowl. Instead they put it on its stand, and it gives light to everyone in the house."

(Matthew 5:16) "In the same way, let your light shine before men that they may see your good deeds and praise your Father in heaven."

Paul says that when you are saved you must also be led, "… because those who are led by the Spirit of God are sons of God" (Romans 8:14). This means that you cannot claim you are born again and yet "do your own thing". As a Christian, you must be led by the Spirit of God.

Another time, Paul said that those led by the Spirit are not under the law; they are not controlled by any regulations set out by the law, but are led by the Spirit of God. "So I say, live by the Spirit, and you will not gratify the desires of the sinful nature. For the sinful nature desires what is contrary to the Spirit and the Spirit what is contrary to the sinful nature. They are in conflict with each other, so that you do not do what you want. But if you are led by the Spirit, you are not under law." (Galatians 5:16–18)

A Christian who fails to be led by the Spirit, who does not reflect on Christ or lead a Christ-like life, brings shame on God, according to the Scriptures, by allowing the enemies of God to blaspheme against the name of the LORD. This is what the prophet Nathan told David, when asked by God to rebuke David after he had sinned with Bathsheba and killed her husband, Uriah. The prophet said: "But because by doing this you have made the enemies of the Lord show utter contempt, the son born to you will die." (2 Samuel 12:14)

Paul said, "You who brag about the law, do you dishonour God by breaking the law? As it is written, 'God's name is blasphemed among the Gentiles because of you. (Romans 2:23–24)

(Isaiah 52:5) "'And now what do I have here?' declares the Lord. 'For my people have been taken away for nothing, and those who rule them mock', declares the Lord. 'And all day long my name is constantly blasphemed.'"

Ask yourself this: does the way you live your life bring shame on the Lord, or does it bring glory to Him?

After we have been born again, there is an obligation to grow to the next stage or step. To reflect on Christ and live a Christ-like life is an essential part of this growth. If one fails to grow in this way, there is a possibility of falling by the wayside or backsliding, and when one has fallen or slid back, it is difficult to climb back according to the writer of Hebrews:

(Hebrews 6:1) "Therefore let us leave the elementary teachings about Christ and go on to maturity, not laying again the foundation of repentance from acts that lead to death, and of faith in God …"

(Hebrews 6:2) "… instruction about baptisms, the laying on of hands, the resurrection of the dead, and eternal judgement."

(Hebrews 6:3) "And God permitting we will do so."

(Hebrews 6:4) "It is impossible for those who have once been enlightened, who have tasted the heavenly gifts, who have shared in the Holy Spirit …"

(Hebrews 6:5) "… who has tasted the goodness of the word of God and the powers of the coming age …"

(Hebrews 6:6) "… if they fall away, to be brought back to repentance because to their loss they are crucifying the Son of God all over again and subjecting him to public disgrace."

Peter said of those who had slipped back, that they are much like a dog returning to his vomit, for Satan will have strengthened his grip on you and will make your return to the right path even more difficult.

(2 Peter 2:22) "Of them the proverbs are true: 'A dog returns to its vomit and, 'A sow that is washed goes back to her wallowing in the mud.'"

(Matthew 12:43) "When an evil spirit comes out of a man, it goes through arid places seeking rest and does not find it."

(Matthew 12:44) "Then it says, 'I will return to the house I left.' When it arrives, it finds the house unoccupied, swept clean and put in order."

(Matthew 12:45) "Then it goes and takes with it seven other spirits more wicked than itself, and they go in and live there. And the final condition of that man is worse than the first. That is how it will be with this wicked generation."

My advice to you all as you read this book is to hold fast to what you have been freely given; cherish your salvation as the most precious gift you have ever owned, and see to it that you live by the standard set by God, just as Paul advises the Philippians' Church:

"Therefore, my dear friends, as you have always obeyed – not only in my presence, but now much more in my absence – continue to work out your salvation with fear and trembling …" (Philippians 2:12)

Another thing I would warn you about is to be careful about your thoughts; what we once believed can have an effect on how we live now, especially when we are alone. In the absence of our Christian leaders and fellow believers, we should focus our attention and devotion even more on Christ so that we do not fall by the wayside or backslide.

I believe that when talking about what sort of life the believer should aspire to, Zacchaeus could be a good example to hold up to all believers. Zacchaeus talks about his life before and after meeting Christ: first, he ensured that nothing could hinder him from seeing Christ and climbed up a sycamore-fig tree; secondly, having come into contact with Jesus, he made restitution that signified and identified him as a new person.

"But Zacchaeus stood up and said to the Lord, 'Look, Lord! Here and now I give half of my possessions to the poor, and if I have cheated anybody out of anything, I will pay back four times the amount.' Jesus said to him, 'Today salvation has come to this house, because this man, too, is a son of Abraham.'" (Luke 19:8–9)

For me, Jesus responds to Zacchaeus' actions in verse 9; for me, here is Jesus saying that this is what it means to be a Christian, a changed person, a person willing to live a life after Him. As we conclude this part of **Be Ye Transformed**, let me remind you that there is no alternative: the Christian life is one way and one way only. It is doing what Christ has asked us to do and not doing what Christ has asked us not to do, for He is the Lord of all. Failure to live by His standards renders you as one who claims to be a Christian only with your mouth, while in your heart you are far away from Him.

The Word of God

Again, let me remind you that to remain saved and to grow, you need the word of God, the food, to nourish your soul. In his first letter, Peter said, "Like new-born babies, crave pure spiritual milk, so that by it you may grow up in your salvation …" (1 Peter 2:2)

Similarly, Paul wrote to the church in Corinth (1 Corinthians 15:1): "Now brothers, I want to remind you of the Gospel I preached to you, which you received and on which you have taken your stand."

(1 Corinthians 15:2) "By this Gospel you are saved, if you hold firmly to the word I preached to you. Otherwise, you have believed in vain."

(1 Corinthians 15:3) "For what I received I passed on to you as of first importance: that Christ died for our sins according to the Scriptures …"

(1 Corinthians 15:4) "… that he was buried, that he was raised on the third day according to the Scriptures …"

Good people or mentors

It is very important to ensure that there are people around you who will be your mentors. Always make sure that you keep good company, being part of a good church will also help you.

(Ephesians 4:11) "It was he who gave some to be apostles, some to be prophets, some to be evangelists and some to be Pastors and teachers …"

(Ephesians 4:12) "… to prepare God's people for works of service, so that the boy of Christ may be built up …"

(Ephesians 4:13) "… until we all reach unity in the faith and in the knowledge of the Son of God and become mature, attaining to the whole measure of the fullness of Christ."

(Ephesians 4:14) "Then we will no longer be infants, tossed back and forth by the waves, and blown here and there by every wind of teaching and by the cunning and craftiness of men in their deceitful scheming."

(Ephesians 4:15) "Instead, speaking the truth in love, we will in all things grow up into him who is the Head, that is, Christ."

(Ephesians 4:16) "From him the whole body, joined and held together by every supporting ligament, grows and builds itself up in love, as each part does its work."

To sustain good nourishment and find reliable mentors, ensure you are around mature Christians and make sure that you are part of a good Bible-based church; all this will be of help to you.

As I said at the previous stage, for many, the progression to being born again is the most difficult of all, because in his deplorable state, man is unable to do anything good for himself.

Furthermore, no one is able to receive salvation or to be born again unless he is willing to leave the old person behind, turn away from the stale food and shackles of his previous life. Although I appreciate that this is not easy, in my personal experience of living a Christian life, as you leave the old man behind, the new you will be born. Trust that when the mind of Christ enters you, just as you leave behind the stale food, the fresh nourishing food that is certain to sustain you will offer itself to you. And as you leave behind the old people that now cannot cope with the new you, so God will deliver to you new people who speak the same language as you, the new man. You lose nothing, but stand to gain everything, believe me.

As Matthew tells us (19:21), Jesus said to the young rich man, "If you want to be perfect, go, sell your possessions and give them to the poor, and you will have treasure in heaven. Then come, follow me." And, "Blessed are the poor in spirit, for theirs is the kingdom of heaven." (Matthew 5:3)

As the old things have passed away and all things have become new, so it is that you cannot grow while you are still holding on to the old things from Stage Zero.

A word of warning here: although the food (the word) and the people (mentors) are very important for your growth as a believer, be very careful about the sort of food you ingest and the people to whom you relate, for receiving the wrong doctrine, listening to bad teachers and false prophets, can hinder your growth.

For example, the Apostle Paul when advising the Colossians' Church said (Colossians 2:8): "See to it that no-one takes you captive through hollow and deceptive philosophy, which depends on human tradition and the basic principles of this world rather than on Christ."

(Colossians 2:9) "For in Christ all the fullness of the Deity lives in bodily form …"

Finally, before you finish reading this stage and proceed to the next one, I want you to examine yourself and answer this question first: "Are you really saved?" If you know deep down that you are not saved, then step towards salvation NOW. Do not delay, I urge you, step forward and follow the steps I give you here. It will be the best decision you have ever made, or will ever make, in your entire life.

If you are certain that you want to be saved or born again at this point, then say this simple prayer with me:

"Heavenly Father I thank you for your only begotten Son Jesus Christ who came to this world to die for our sins. I believe with my heart and, therefore, confess with my mouth that you raised Him from the dead. I now accept Him as my personal Lord and Saviour and ask that Jesus Christ come into my life and live with me for all eternity." Thank you Lord that I am now saved and truly born again according to your word. Amen."

Now, if you have genuinely spoken this prayer with your mouth and in your heart then I am also rejoicing with you, and welcome you wholeheartedly into the family of God, the greatest and best-loved family in the whole world.

Jesus said, "I tell you that in the same way there will be more rejoicing in heaven over one sinner who repents than over ninety-nine righteous persons who do not need to repent." (Luke 15:7)

This quotation brings to mind another powerful song we used to sing in Ghana, which uses the same powerful words of the Scripture above. We would sing this song joyfully whenever people responded to the call of God for salvation during our crusades years ago. The song went:

> "There is rejoicing in the presence of the angels of God over one sinner who repents."

Stage Two: Christian Growth

Having been born again, which is the best thing that can ever happen to anybody, it is expected that as a believer you will now grow, just as the newborn baby is expected to grow naturally. Therefore, whether you were born again before or after reading this book, your next step is Stage Two: Christian Growth, where growth is paramount for every believer.

By this stage, the born-again believer, the transformed man, begins to take nourishment and maturity from the word of God. For those believers who do not or cannot read the word, it filters into their minds through what they hear from others. For the literate, however, they may gain knowledge through what they hear and read; they should ensure that they make it a point of their new born-again life that they study and practice the word on their own.

In his first letter Peter (1 Peter 2:1) offers the new born-again believers some advice, saying:

"Therefore get rid of yourselves of all malice and all deceit, hypocrisy, envy, and slander of every kind."

(1 Peter 2:2) "Like new-born babies, crave spiritual milk, so that by it you may grow up in your salvation …"

(1 Peter 2:3) "Now that you have tasted that the Lord is good."

In order to grow, the born-again Christian must do away with everything that will make his or her growth more difficult. He will feed only on the word of God, which is his spiritual milk to build up strength and maturity. If you are a believer, new or old, I want to emphasise again that, in order to be able to grow in Christ as is required by God, you must do away with malice and all deceit, hypocrisy, envy, and slander of every kind, else these will hinder your growth.

Paul, on the other hand, refers to the born-again man who fails to grow as "the carnal man". In 1 Corinthians 3:1–3. He said:

"And I, brethren, could not speak to you as to spiritual *people* but as to carnal, as to babes in Christ. I fed you with milk and not with solid food; for until now you were not able *to receive it*, and even now, you are still not able; for you are still carnal. For where *there are* envy, strife and divisions among you, are you not carnal and behaving like *mere* men?"

In this stage of man note that Paul refers to them as "brethren", which means they are brothers, they are born-again, members of God's family, but carnal. This means that they are fleshly, that is, that they are born again, but controlled by the flesh instead of the Spirit. These people call themselves Christians, but do not live by the direction of the Holy Spirit; like the natural man, they are controlled by their five senses.

Paul says that he cannot relate to these Christians as Spiritual believers because they are still babes, but he means this in opposition to the notion that every believer, like natural babies, are supposed to grow after receiving Christ, for He sees these believers as still acting like children and behaving immaturely. As Paul points out, where envy, strife and divisions exist among us, we are carnal and behaving like mere or ordinary men.

At this stage, therefore, those who are born again will be either illiterate or literate, developing their desires to feed on the word of God. His or her learning will enable growth through listening, reading or studying the word in person. As it is the desire of every child to be like his or her elder brother or sister in the natural world. I am amazed therefore that people do not desire to grow in the Lord when they are born again. For when we are born again, we become spiritual new-born babies that are expected to grow in strength and maturity.

When I was a child, like any other child, I wanted to be like my big brother and sister because they had more freedom than I was allowed. They were allowed to do things that were forbidden for me, allowed to go out on their own even without much resistance or interruption from our parents; they could buy food and clothes for themselves with their own money, which they had earned from doing petty jobs, while I was still dependent on my parents.

As a boy, one of my greatest desires was to grow quickly and become like my father. I wanted to be treated respectfully like him, especially when we were having our evening meal as he would always get the most meat! The worst thing of all was seeing the small portion given to me against that of my elder brother. He always had a bigger portion than mine. At that time, little did I understand the significance of the Akan proverb that says, "To be a man or adult is a bitter experience; a great responsibility."

Just like me as a boy, I have seen many young people rushing to become adults in life, maybe not because they wanted to get a bigger portion of meat, as I desired, but for other reasons. My question is this: do we desire as believers to grow in our spiritual transformation just as we do in our physical stature; do we crave to know more about God and to be able to take spiritual responsibility?

Your answer is as good as mine, and as we proceed further, your answer to this question will be a great help to your spiritual transformation.

In the same way that when a child fails to grow physically people worry that s/he is disabled; likewise, one becomes spiritually disabled if one fails to grow in the Lord after being born again. How sad it is that some people never grow up when they say they have been born again. The writer of Hebrews says:

(Hebrews 6:1) "Therefore, let us leave the elementary teachings about Christ and go to maturity, not laying again the foundation of repentance from acts that lead to death, and of faith in God …"

(Hebrews 6:2) "… instruction about baptisms, the laying on of hands, the resurrection of the dead, and eternal judgement."

According to the two Scriptures above, certain teachings or doctrines are elementary, and should form the basis of all believers' faith. These basics include the importance of faith; the foolishness of trying to be saved by good deeds; the meaning of baptism and spiritual gifts; the facts about Resurrection and eternal life; how to be born again; and the assurance of salvation.

Believers are expected to move beyond these elementary teachings and grasp a more complete understanding of their faith. In so doing, they should grow to maturity in their deepened sense of knowledge. Mature Christians should be teaching new Christians the basics; and while doing so, should be acting on what they know, so that they learn even more about the meanings of God's word. Believers should depend on Christ and live effectively for Him.

I find that many Christians are still spiritual babies because of their deeds. Despite being Christians for many years, they fail to develop or mature in God.

Paul addresses the Corinthians' Church as infants because of their deeds, "Brothers," he says, "I could not address you as spiritual but as worldly – mere infants in Christ. I gave you milk, not solid food, for you were not yet ready for it. Indeed, you are still not ready. You are still worldly.

"For since there is jealousy and quarrelling among you, are you not worldly? Are you not acting like mere men? For when one says, 'I follow Paul,' and another, 'I follow Apollos,' are you not mere men?" (1 Corinthians 3:1–4)

Paul is castigating the Corinthians by telling them that they are still children; they are showing their immaturity by quarrelling and allowing envy, strife and divisions among them. He tells them that they are immature Christians, who like babies require milk instead of the solid food they should require as mature adults.

In this respect, I say to you all, both as individual believers and collectively as church goers, all those who allow themselves to be bogged down with these same elementary issues in their lives or between themselves, irrespective of how many years they may have been in Christ, they are all still babies.

Ask yourselves this: if Paul visited you in person or dropped into your church as he did to the Corinthians' Church, could you look honestly at your actions and behaviour and know what food he should offer you? Would it be milk, infant food, or solid food fit for a mature adult Christian?

Just as Paul said to the Corinthians' Church, I suggest to you in much the same way that many believers are still immature babies who, although old in the Lord, still need milk rather than solid food. If you still envy your brother, or if you are the reason of division in your family or church, then you are one of these people to whom Paul was speaking.

As I have mentioned previously, at each stage you will need wholesome food and/or people (a mentor) to help you to move forward. I know that some food and some people at certain stages will not be relevant, whereas at other stages what was previously irrelevant will become extremely useful. The relevance of good food and wholesome people, therefore, cannot be over-estimated for the growth and maturity of a born-again Christian. Some activities and people with which you might be involved are faith-killers. They will not be helpful if you desire to grow in your Christian life;

therefore, you must leave them behind no matter how much you like, or even love them.

Anyone who fails to mature through the stages becomes extremely vulnerable to all sorts of teachings and doctrines. They can easily be driven away from God by them. Just as Paul says, the steady growth of every born-again Christian is essential:

(Ephesians 4:14) "Then we will no longer be infants, tossed back and forth by the waves, and blown here and there by every wind of teaching and by the cunning and craftiness of men in their deceitful scheming."

(Ephesians 4:15) "Instead, speaking the truth in love, we will in all things grow up into him who is the Head, that is, Christ."

And, again, in Hebrews:

(Hebrews 5:12) "In fact, though by this time you ought to be teachers, you need someone to teach you the elementary truths of God's word all over again."

(Hebrews 5:13) "Anyone who lives on milk, being still an infant, is not acquainted with the teaching about righteousness."

(Hebrews 5:14) "But solid food is for the mature, who by constant use have trained themselves to distinguish good from evil."

In much the same way, take the many people that today fill up our churches and have been Christians for many years. Are they not supposed to be teachers and mentors of the young ones? Instead, many are still infants themselves, they have failed to grow, and this lack of growth causes themselves and others unnecessary instability. For as they move from church to church, whereby such and such is a member of this church today, and another by tomorrow, they take with them the immature infants. In a supposedly mature Christian, this swapping and changing is a sure sign of immaturity, because immature Christians follow and are carried away by any doctrine or teaching.

Against this act of fickle indecision, in his concluding words, Peter advises his readers to be on their guard so that they may not be carried away by those who are not ready to change. He counsels that there is always room for change:

(2 Peter 3:17) "Therefore, dear friends, since you already know this, be on your guard so that you may not be carried away by the error of lawless men and fall from your secure position."

(2 Peter 3:18) "But grow in the grace and knowledge of our Lord and Saviour Jesus Christ. To him be glory both now and forever! Amen."

How can I grow as a Christian?

Many ask the question: "How can I grow as a Christian into maturity as required by God?" True, there is much work to do, but there is hope and guidance in the Bible, which you should study well, meditating on the word of God. As you read *Be Ye Transformed*, contemplate on it and learn from it. You will certainly be nourished and grow as a Christian in your spiritual transformation.

As Paul said (2 Corinthians 5:17) "Therefore, if anyone is in Christ, he is a new creation; the old has gone, the new has come!"

Christianity means change; when you become Christian, you should not remain the same; a Christian is a sinner saved or changed by grace. Therefore, as you read *Be Ye Transformed*, I would like you first to examine yourself: ask yourself if you are the same person or whether you have changed since you became Christian, or were born again.

As I mentioned earlier, just as every parent would like their babies to grow and become mature enough to take responsibility in the physical world, in much the same way, God wants His children to grow and take responsibility for their spiritual growth.

It is a big problem for all parents if their child fails to grow naturally. I don't think my parents or your parents would be happy if you or I were still the same as we were when we were one or two years old. It is the same with God; He is disappointed and worried when His children fail to grow.

For God, maturity is an important requirement from His children; many may not know it, but every Christian is born again (having first been born physically of our parents, and been re-born in the Spirit of God).

Before any of us can be successful Christians, we must first learn the rules and regulations of Christian growth. This is essential. There are always rules for everything, and, through Paul, I now offer you guidance on how to grow as a Christian. This guidance will enhance your spiritual, Christian growth.

Paul said to Timothy:

(2 Timothy 2:5) "Similarly, if anyone competes as an athlete, he does not receive the victor's crown unless he competes according to the rules."

If you want to grow, you need to know and respect the rules for growth set up by God, otherwise you cannot compete; you cannot mature in that contest. As a fan of all sports, I respect that they all have rules and regulations. Going against the rules can result in injury, loss of points, disqualification and even in being stripped of medals.

No matter how fast you can run, if you leave your lane or commit a false start, it will almost certainly lead to disqualification. The American Four-by-Four Relay team had its gold medal confiscated because one of the athletes ran out of his lane. A renowned athlete was also stripped of his gold medal after it was decided he had broken the rules by taking a banned drug. Another UK athlete was disqualified for a false start by the athletes' federation. In boxing, punching below the belt is against the rules and can result in the loss of points. In football, a vital gaol can be disallowed because of the offside rule. No matter how strong a weightlifter thinks he is, he risks breaking his back if he doesn't use the correct posture and procedure for weight-lifting.

The common mission of every believer is to grow into maturity as we journey to heaven. Paul, knowing that Christians would be tempted on their journey by Satan – who always wants to deter believers from reaching their goal – gave four biblical directives to assist believers in growth and maturity. As we have seen above, Christian growth is not optional: it is a requirement that every believer must pursue if s/he wants to mature.

I hope as you read the directives below you will be encouraged to take them seriously and apply them to your own life. The failure of many believers on their journey to Christ is not that they doubt the truth of God's word, but that they fail to apply God's word to their own life. What I am trying to tell you as you read the rules is this: do not simply read what they say, but apply what the rules say to the way you live your life. As you do so, you will grow, and the results of your determination will become abundantly clear.

1. Self-denial

(1 Corinthians 9:24) "Do you not know that in a race all the runners run, but only one gets the prize? Run in such as to get the prize."

(1 Corinthians 9:25) "Everyone who competes in the games goes into strict training. They do it to get a crown that will not last; but we do it to get a crown that will last forever."

(1 Corinthians 9:26) "Therefore I do not run like a man running aimlessly; I do not fight like a man beating the air."

(1 Corinthians 9:27) "No, I beat my body and make it my slave so that after I have preached to others, I myself will not be disqualified for the prize."

In the first part of Paul's teaching on how to grow as a Christian, he compares our Christian life to a race. He says, "As everyone needs a vision to accomplish a mission the 'Plan' is to deny ourselves of many things in order to do our best."

Paul says that winning a race requires purpose and discipline. He uses this illustration to explain that the Christian life takes hard work, self-denial and tough preparation. As Christians, we are running towards our heavenly reward. The essential disciplines of fasting and prayer, Bible study, and practising the word will equip us to run with strength and stamina. Furthermore, we should not be only spectators, simply cheering others on, we should be a part of the team, part of the race. He says that winning the race – our spiritual progress being the goal – will depend on how strictly we train and discipline ourselves.

Most Christians do not practise full self-control; for many anything goes, they act like loose cannons, out-of-control vehicles without brakes, and cannot control themselves. You cannot win a race with this kind of character. Jesus Christ set out the conditions for His disciples, and indeed set out rules for all believers that wish to become His disciples. To me, in the context of this book, these same conditions apply on our journey to Christian growth and maturity.

1. "Then Jesus said to his disciples, 'if anyone would come after me, he must deny himself and take up his cross and follow me. For whoever wants to save his life will lose it, but whoever loses his life for me will find it.'" (Matthew 16:24–25)

2. "If anyone comes to me and does not hate his father and mother, his wife and children, his brothers and sisters – yes, even his own life – he cannot be my disciple." (Luke 14:26)

3. "In the same way, any of you who do not give up everything he has cannot be my disciple." (Luke 14:33)

What is Jesus saying here? He is saying that anyone who wants to be His disciple must be ready to deny themselves certain material comforts and things of the flesh. This might include leaving behind those whom we love, those who for one reason or another may hinder our growth. Remember what I said earlier in relation to spiritual food, the word of God, that there are certain people or mentors who will be very important in our walk with God, but others in our Christian life that will not be relevant as we proceed. At certain stages in your growth – in your spiritual transformation – therefore, you will enjoy witnessing your growth, and with the devil behind them, there will be others attempting to hinder your journey.

Jesus not only set out conditions to become His disciple, but He also offered a reward for self-denial, which in the context of this book I hope will encourage believers to grow to maturity. Listen to what Jesus said:

"'I tell you the truth,' Jesus said to them, 'no-one who has left home or wife or brothers or parents or children for the sake of the kingdom of God will fail to receive many times as much in this age and, in the age to come, eternal life.'" (Luke 18:29–30)

Here, Jesus tells His disciples and, indeed all believers, that in order to follow Him they must deny themselves and take up their cross. What He means is that all those who wish to be disciples must put away all desires of the flesh and be ready to bear whatever pain results from self-denial, refusing to follow anything or anybody that entices one to do evil.

The cross is a metaphor for the pain that Jesus said one must bear as a result of reproaching his father and mother, his wife and children, his brothers and sisters, and even his own life. Does this mean Jesus is preaching hatred or disobedience toward our parents? No! What He means is that when you are tempted to return to people you know are a bad influence on you, or should you be compelled to return to activities or places from which you have been saved, which are contrary to the word of God, when even your own body may tempt you back to the wrong path away from the word of God, then you must be bold enough to say "No!" You must exercise self-control.

To sum up: in order to mature, the believer must be able to say "No!" He must be able to deny anything or anybody that might cause him to go against the word of God, no matter how hard or painful it might be.

The cross before Resurrection

Jesus will rise from the dead in three days, but before the Resurrection, which shows His power over sin and death, Jesus must first go to the cross. Without the Resurrection, His virgin birth, sinless life and His atoning, His death would have been in vain.

The Resurrection crowns the Life of Christ, but before the Resurrection, Christ had to suffer the pain of the cross: before any victory in life, there must first be self-denial.

Israel was told that they would possess the Promised Land; the land that flowed with milk and honey, but first they all must leave and forget Egypt and go through the wilderness, the place of suffering, to be humble in the sight of God for forty years. It is clear in Exodus that those whose hearts were still in Egypt had sinned against God, and the result was the death of all of them, so that only Joshua and Caleb of their generation reached the Promised Land.

It is the same for believers who fail to experience the cross of their lives: there will be no resurrection for them. Similarly, believers that fail to experience the wilderness cannot enter the Promised Land. Believers can only grow to maturity when they separate themselves from the things of the world.

Athletes, and those who want to lose weight to compete at a high level, deny themselves many types of food and drink in order to keep their weight down and compete at their best. In the same way, Christians who want to grow in God must deny themselves of many things that will be unhelpful to their spiritual growth. Some of our friends, acquaintances and habits have to go, therefore, although, often, relinquishing these things is not easy.

The author of Hebrews tells us:

(Hebrews 12:1) "Therefore, since we are surrounded by such a great cloud of witnesses, let us throw off everything that hinders and the sin that so easily entangles, and let us run with perseverance the race marked out for us."

(Hebrews 12:2) "Let us fix our eyes on Jesus, the author and the perfecta of our faith, who for the joy set before him endured the cross, scorning its shame, and sat down at the right hand of the throne of God."

What is this saying to us? It is saying that growing to maturity takes a lot of effort and dedication. We must be ready to give up every sin and every worldly attribute of the physical life; leaving behind anybody or anything that will get in the way of our goal. We must leave behind those who try to distract us from our focus on Christ, for example, as it will cause us to lose the race. We can only do this when we are in tune with the Holy Spirit; He will help us to focus and resist all distractions.

I have never seen an athlete ready to run, a footballer ready to play in the field, or a boxer ready to fight in the ring wearing a business suit or a heavy overcoat, have you? They will wear appropriate clothing: a light and suitable outfit that will assist them in doing their best. Why can't believers who want to grow or win the Christian life-race, do the same then?

As you read this book, some of you may well ask, "Why do we have to suffer and deny ourselves of things like athletes?"

The answer to this is that the prize is infinitely greater than that offered to athletes who win an Olympic event. The glory of his or her prize of a gold, silver or bronze medal does not last for long, but for us, our "crown will last forever." (1 Corinthians 9:25)

Sometimes I do find it very hard to understand why even some very devout and good Christians do so well at observing all the regulations that keep their physical body fit – they will do anything required of them to gain a high position and status in life – but fail abysmally to abide by the rules and regulations that will keep them fit spiritually. Their spiritual life, however, will supersede any achievements they can possibly make in the physical realm.

To be able to grow as a Christian you are required to deny yourself of things that are not profitable to you in your spiritual life, and distance yourself from people that will hinder your spiritual growth, even though it might not be easy.

A child does not mature into adulthood in a day. A child progresses through different stages and development from baby to toddler, from toddler to child, from child to adolescent, from adolescent to young adult, and finally a mature adult.

In the exact same way, the believer's growth to maturity does not happen in a day, and is fraught with challenges. Progress comes not only through determination, but also by the believer's willingness to grow, as well as encouragement from others (mentors). For example, when a child is learning how to walk, there are times he stumbles and falls, hurting himself in the process. Gradually, however, with persistence, he perfects the art of walking. How? Through his persistence, determination and the encouragement of those who care for him.

My son in the Lord, Pastor Paul Tom Kanga of the Apostolic Church, Cameroon, was preaching once about the progressive growth of a Christian. During his sermon he said, "If I see a child less than one year old who is supposed to be crawling and he starts to run, I will also run away, in fear, because it is abnormal for a child of that age – it is impossible. Normally a child learns to run gradually, after he has mastered crawling, toddling and when walking." He continued: "It has not been easy for me in my process of growth; it has taken the grace of God and my willingness to grow. In my early years, there were times I fell like a child into those things from which I have been saved, the things of the flesh, those things considered wrong and unworthy for a believer to do. Thank God, when I fell I did not stay down, but I got up by the grace of God, and continued to grow on the right path. To be precise and to be honest, throughout 1975, the year I was born again, even though the zeal to follow Christ was there, there was a struggle between my spirit and my flesh. Life was often up and down, until 1976, when I found myself totally committed and fully subjected to the will of God. From then on, I experienced that the 'old me' was replaced with life in Jesus Christ, and now He is living in me. If you are struggling now, I assure you that the grace of God will do the same for you and even more. The question is: are you willing to change and therefore grow?"

While reflecting on my own journey into maturity I see that many things came and went. During the different stages of my life, I also saw many people come and go. Some left me, while I had to leave others behind because I wanted to move on and grow. Those who wanted to move on with me, because they had the same goal as me, are still with me today, but those who had different ideas and could not cope with the new me, have all gone.

There were so many things that I had to stop doing, and although it was often difficult to stop doing these things, I knew it was not good for me to carry on doing them as a Christian. I remember one particularly difficult decision I had to make in my early Christian life: One night I cried like a baby when I had to tell a girl that I had decided to end our relationship because I had seen the light and could not cope any longer with the sin. What made matters worse was that the girl began to cry also, because I had asked to end the relationship although I asked that we remain friends.

I ended that relationship and stopped many other things as well, because my life in Christ was more valuable to me than any other thing the world could offer. I was young in the Lord and it was very hard, but even so, I was willing to do what was right. The grace of God was sufficient strength to enable me to subdue the desire of the flesh. I was able to end the relationship and make the decision to live the right way with God. Praise God!

Some years later, God gave me my lovely wife, Lydia, a real companion and compliment to me, who restored to me all I needed from a woman. We are blessed with three children between us, and I have never regretted our lives being bonded together through marriage for the past twenty-six (26) years. She has been an inspiration and a great support to this day, helping me to write this book. We have gone through many challenges together and thank God that, together, we are still growing.

In another incident, I once had to ignore the advice given to me by someone for whom I had enormous respect. I had gone to him for advice about a temptation I was facing as a young Christian, which was causing me great physical pain. This is what he said to me and I will quote his exact words: "Kwadwo [the name given to every male born on Monday from the Akan tribe in Ghana], the only remedy to this problem you are facing is to find yourself a woman, only that will only help you to ease the pain."

Still in great pain, I left this man's house thinking to myself that I was prepared to die rather than defile myself and sin against God, and from that day on, I knew that this man was no longer fit or able to give me counsel. Although in the past this man had helped me, I knew that now, looking towards the goal I wanted to reach, he could not help me get there.

My friends, at some time you may also have to deny a friendship or admit that you have lost respect for someone. You may even have to face that you have lost sympathy for someone, if you want to reach that higher level.

2. Forget the past: Put all your effort into pressing forward

(Philippians 3:13) "Brothers, I do not consider myself yet to have taken hold of it. But one thing I do: Forgetting what is behind and straining towards what is ahead …"

(Philippians 3:14) "I press on towards the goal to win the prize for which God has called me heavenwards in Christ Jesus."

Again, in his letter to the Philippians' Church, Paul compares the life of a committed Christian to a race, but this time the "Plan" is to:

- Forget the past and move forward;
- Do so with all effort and energy;
- To win the race.

Forgetting the past is one of the hardest things for most people to do. It was so for Paul when he wrote the letter to the Philippians, where, in spite of all his achievements as an Apostle, even Paul does not yet consider himself to have let go of the past. In other words, even Paul had not yet won the race, but in his plan to do so, he tries to forget the past that he knows could hinder his progress or growth in the Lord. As a great persecutor of the Church, who also played a vital part in the martyrdom of Stephen, Paul's ability to forget his past misdemeanours, and look towards a future with hope, is of critical importance.

Consider these verses on how Paul, in his past, contributed to the stoning of Stephen, a misdemeanour which could have been a great hindrance to his growth in God, had he allowed it to be.

(Acts 7:58) "[They] dragged him out of the city and began to stone him. Meanwhile, the witnesses laid their clothes at the feet of the young man named Saul.

(Acts 7:59) "While they were stoning him, Stephen prayed, 'Lord Jesus receive my spirit.'

(Acts 8:1) "And Saul was there, giving approval to his death. On that day a great persecution broke out against the church at Jerusalem, and all except the apostles were scattered throughout Judea and Samaria.

(Acts 9:1–2) "Meanwhile, Saul was still breathing out murderous threats against the Lord's disciples. He went to the high priest and asked him for letters to the synagogues in Damascus, so that if he found any there who belonged to the Way, whether men or women, he might take them as prisoners to Jerusalem."

In short, Paul knew he could not do anything for the Lord if he did not try to forget these and other atrocious acts against the church. In fact, in his own testimony following his mysterious conversion, he answers Jesus' question: he said, "We all fell to the ground, and I heard a voice saying to me in Aramaic, 'Saul, Saul, why do you persecute me? It is hard for you to kick against the goads.'" (Acts 26:14)

Worst of all, is that even when Paul started preaching Christ after his conversion people were running from him, and others were accusing him and referring him to his past. Paul did not allow any of these taunts, jibes and accusations to deter him from moving forward however.

The Bible says in (Acts 9:27) "But Barnabas took him and brought him to the apostles. He told them how Saul on his journey had seen the Lord and that the Lord had spoken to him, and how in Damascus he had preached fearlessly in the name of Jesus.

(Acts 9:28) "So Saul stayed with them and moved about freely in Jerusalem.

(Acts 9:29) "He talked and debated with the Grecian Jews, but they tried to kill him."

Thus, it is so for everybody that one hinders progress in life if one cannot forget the past. Do you think that if Paul had allowed all these setbacks from his past to take a hold of him he would have been able to do what he accomplished for the Lord? I don't think so.

Like Paul, I believe that I would not be where I am now, preaching and teaching God's word and writing books, if I had still held on to my memories of what I used to do before I was a Christian, and in the early years of my life in Christ. I am able to move on because I have learned to put the past behind me. You can also do the same if you learn to forget the past and move on.

The motivation in all competitions is to win. An athlete who finishes the race last would have been better off not competing in the first place, for there is no reward to those who finish last. To achieve the first three places, more effort is needed to run faster than the other athletes do. Looking at the faces of some athletes during a race, their efforts are often discernable; the determination to win is visible on their faces.

It is never easy to deny yourself something you desire, want to do or somebody you want to see, but with determination, your mission of winning the race is in sight. Trust me that, with determination, you can resist reminiscing and dwelling on the past. Never look back: athletes that look back constantly often end up losing concentration and the race! Constantly looking back allows the other runners to close up on them, and then often, to overtake them.

Like Paul, we all have a past: sins we have committed and mistakes we have made; squandered opportunities; failed promises; lost jobs; failed dreams, broken marriages or relationships even, and all these "failures" can be obstacles and setbacks to our future growth and spiritual transformation. However, if we are able to put the past behind us and forget what has been; know and have faith in God that all things have become new;

press forward in our new life and focus on the goal of winning the prize for which God has called us heavenward in Christ Jesus, we will attain our everlasting reward. Just as Paul experienced, certain people may try to remind you of your past, taunt you, and say or do hurtful things to you. However, as Paul says, we should put every effort into forgetting the past, ignoring those who hark back to it, if it is our desire to grow or to be transformed.

Another way to forget the past is to forgive and forget. To be able to forgive and forget what others have done against you, or for that matter what you have perpetrated against others, is an important step towards growth. Those who are unable to forgive and forget, who dwell constantly on the past – a habit of many – will inevitably experience **bitterness**, which is one of the most insidious barriers to growth that there is.

The writer of Hebrews gives a very strict warning concerning bitterness (Hebrews 12:15): "See to it that no-one misses the grace of God and that no bitter root grows up to cause trouble and defile many."

It is said that, "A little drop of water makes a mighty ocean", but if one fails to deal with a small bitterness it can grow to become a mighty ocean, a vast expanse that becomes an obstacle and hindrance to your relationship with God. Jesus said:

(Matthew 6:14) "For if you forgive men, when they sin against you, your heavenly Father, will also forgive you.

(Matthew 6:15) "But if you do not forgive men their sins, your Father will not forgive your sins."

I once heard a man saying that his mind was like the Bible, in the sense that the Bible's words were long lasting. Therefore, according to this man, he would never be able to forget when someone had offended him. If you are like this man, you had better change, because you are not doing yourself any good. You must not follow this man's attitude, as he is deluded in his thinking.

To forgive someone who has hurt you is a very hard thing to do, and that is why you need to expend effort and energy in trying to forgive and forget.

I cannot deny that even I have found it hard to forgive and forget in the past when someone has offended me. The worst of it is when you hear that someone very close to you or someone you expected to defend or care for you, as you would do for them, is in part to blame for your trouble. If you hear that someone you once trusted has been undermining you or has betrayed you, it is very, very hard to forget and forget.

The word from the Master, however, should make it easier, He says, "And whenever you stand praying, if you have anything against anyone, forgive him that your Father in heaven may also forgive you your trespasses. But if you do not forgive, neither will your Father in heaven forgive your trespasses." (Mark 11:25–26)

This means that someone's mistake or sin against you could cause you to sin against them also, which would mean that you also risk sinning against God. This would be a hindrance to receiving your blessing from God, and so for this reason alone, you must forgive and forget and make an effort to avoid those people or actions that represent a stumbling block on your path to growth.

Here is another example: Jesus said (Matthew 11:12): "From the days of John the Baptist until now, the kingdom of heaven has been forcefully advancing, and forceful men lay hold of it."

Which means, therefore, that in order to grow as Christians, we need to forget the past and press forward to reach what is ahead of us and our ultimate goal: the day when we come face-to-face with Jesus in heaven.

Now while we have been reflecting on the importance of forgiving and forgetting, I should mention the vainglorious: those people that dwell and talk constantly about their past glories, those who never seek to achieve new goals, or develop themselves further, but hark on constantly about past-achievements.

These people never grow either. While it is good to talk about what the Lord is using you for, or did through you ten years ago, do you not think it is more relevant to talk about what He is doing through you today? What was relevant back then may not be relevant today; what people admired you for then may not be admirable today. While I agree that it is good to have past testimonies or glories, it is not better than having current projects worth testimony is it? Think about that!

Lot's wife was unable to escape with her family because her heart was still in the past. She could not pursue what was ahead and so turned into a pillar of salt. She and her family were given the chance to run for their lives, but because her heart was in the past, it kept her back.

(Genesis 19:17) "As soon as they had brought them out, one of them said: 'Flee for your lives! Don't look back, and don't stop anywhere in the plain! Flee to the mountains or you will be swept away!'"

(Genesis 19:26) "But Lot's wife looked back, and she became a pillar of salt."

In order to grow you must let go of many things from your past to progress with God, you cannot proceed while you still hold on to the old man and his deeds. Jesus said:

(Matthew 6:24) "No-one can serve two masters. Either he will hate the one and love the other, or he will be devoted to the one and despise the other. You cannot serve both God and Money."

Take the children of Israel whose story was recorded by the psalmist. They became stagnant and hung up their harps, the instrument that connected them to God. Having done that, all they could do was weep because then they kept looking back and reminiscing. At that point, when their enemies realised that they had abandoned their relationship with their God, they took advantage of their vulnerability, making fun of them and asking them to sing to them one of the songs they used to sing in Zion. In other words, they were taunting, "where is your God?" As told in Psalm 137:1–4, "By the rivers of Babylon we sat and wept when we remembered Zion. There on the poplars we hung our harps, for there our captors asked us for songs, our tormentors demanded songs of joy; they said, 'Sing us one of the songs of Zion!'"

Remember that constantly looking back and reminiscing about the past, rather than looking forward and celebrating the future, will hinder your progress and leave you vulnerable to your enemy's taunts. As encouragement, allow me to prophesy to you with these words of the prophet:

"'The glory of this present house will be greater than the glory of the former house,' says the Lord Almighty. 'And in this place I will grant peace,' declares the Lord Almighty." (Haggai 2:9)

No matter what you have lost or what went wrong, no matter who ever failed you, forget it! Forget all past disappointments, failures, mistakes, and even past glories and just look to tomorrow with the hope that, with God still on the throne, the glory of the future house shall be greater than the former, Praise God!

To conclude this part, I would like you to take for yourself these prophetic words from the prophet Isaiah:

> "Do not remember the former things, Nor consider the things of old. Behold, I will do a new thing, Now it shall spring forth; Shall you not know it? I will even make a road in the wilderness *And* rivers in the desert. The beast of the field will honour Me, The jackals and the ostriches, Because I give waters in the wilderness *And* rivers in the desert, To give drink to My people, My chosen." (Isaiah 43:18–20)

3. Endurance in the fight
(2 Timothy 4:7) "I have fought the good fight, I have finished the race, I have kept the faith."

(2 Timothy 4:8) "Now there is in store for me the crown of righteousness, which the Lord, the righteous judge, will award to me on that day – and not only me, but also to all who have longed for his appearing."

This time Paul compares our Christian life to a boxing match. The "Plan" this time is to fight long and hard until the battle is won. It is easy to give up, quit or run from the devil or problems, but this is not a good strategy in our fight against the enemy. In order to guarantee victory we must possess endurance and patience; we must have faith that Christ is on our side.

Under no circumstances must believers give up or lose hope. After all, Christians have everything it takes to win all battles of this world, because we have been provided with the word of God, which holds all the answers to all life's questions, and offers solutions to any problems that arise.

Yet, as believers, we must admit that the Christian life is a fight against the devil and the evil things of this world. The devil is always goading believers into a fight because he wants to hinder them in their process of spiritual transformation and make their journey to heaven as difficult as possible. The devil also wants to deprive believers of the enjoyment of God's blessings, which He has given us to enjoy here on earth.

To win this fight, Paul uses his own experience to encourage his son, Timothy, in the Lord. He encourages Timothy and all believers to fight long and hard; he insists that believers should never give up until the fight is won; Paul promotes perseverance, the result of which is seen in our receiving the crown of righteousness, which our Lord the righteous judge, will award to everyone on that day when we see Him face-to-face in heaven.

The writer of Hebrews says:

(Hebrews 10:35) "So do not throw away your confidence; it will be richly rewarded."

(Hebrews 10:36) "You need to persevere so that when you have done the will of God, you will receive what he has promised."

The message here is this: having done all that we need to do in order to grow, we must also exercise patience in the knowledge that we will come face-to-face with the Lord in heaven. In our race against sin and self-indulgence, Christ is there to see us through, so long as we do not give up.

Again, Paul counsels believers to put on the "full armour of God" in order that we are able to take our stand against the devil and win the fight (Ephesians 6:10–17), Christ is our armour! He represents all the armour Paul lists, and with Him, we have all that it takes to overcome the devil.

- He is our belt of truth. In John (14:6) He says, "I am the way and the truth and the life. No-one comes to the Father except through me". He is the image of the invisible God, the firstborn over all creation. (Colossians 1:15). Jesus is the reality of all that God says He is; the only way or the bridge to God, the truth every man must know. As the belt is worn around the waist, with Him, all the weapons that are needed to fight the enemy hold together.

- He is our breastplate of righteousness to protect out heart. Paul says, "This righteousness from God comes through faith in Jesus Christ to all who believe. There is no difference" (Romans 3:22). Without Christ, therefore, no one can live righteously.

- He is our Gospel of peace fitted to our feet. "For to us a child is born, to us a son is given, and the government will be on his shoulders. And he will be called Wonderful Counsellor, Mighty God, Everlasting Father, and Prince of Peace" (Isaiah 9:6). With Him, we have peace with God.

- He is our shield of faith; with Him, we extinguish all the flaming arrows of the evil one.

With Jesus, we may hold the conviction that all that God has promised and everything we have asked of Him according to His word, is already done. Everything becomes possible because we act on what we believe, just as Abraham did:

- "Against all hope, Abraham in hope believed and so became the father of many nations, just as it had been said to him, 'So shall your offspring be.' Without weakening in his faith, he faced the fact that his body was as good as dead – since he was about a hundred years old – and that Sarah's womb was also dead. Yet he did not waver through unbelief regarding the promise of God, but was strengthened in his faith and gave glory to God, being fully persuaded that God had power to do what he had promised." (Romans 4:18–21)

- He is our helmet of salvation. With Him, our salvation is safe and secure, and well protected. As our heads are covered with the helmet of salvation, our minds are kept focused only on Him; the only way to eternal life: "Salvation is found in no-one else, for there is no other name under heaven given to men by which we must be saved." (Acts 4:12; more in verse 10–11)

- Finally, He is our defensive weapon, sword of the Spirit, which is the word of God. With the word of God at hand, we can fight any problems or situations we may face in life. Jesus Christ is the true example of defeating the devil with God's word: in the three temptations He faced from the devil in the wilderness, His response was as it is written. Jesus demonstrated to us the importance and the effectiveness of God's word.

When your eyes are on Him, you become strong in the Lord. In His mighty power, you have the full armour of God and, because you have the full armour of God, you can take your stand against any of the devil's schemes when the day of evil comes. When we come against the rulers, against the authorities of evil in the heavenly realm, we are sure to win any fight. Jesus is all you need, He is both our defensive and offensive weapon; with Him in focus, believers can defend themselves and fight against any of the devil's onslaughts.

Never, ever give up, but fight to the end. As a believer, never allow anybody or anything to take your eyes away from Jesus. If you lose sight of Him, you have lost all that it takes to survive. For He is well able to take care of any problems you will face in this life. As Jesus came to suffer, so He is well prepared to help those who also suffer.

Recently, I came to the realisation that if there is anything at all for which I have to commend Satan, it is this: he is more committed and reliable in his campaign to defeat believers than anyone I have ever seen or heard about. He is in business twelve hours a day, twelve hours a night, and seven days a week (24/7). The devil never rests and, therefore, it takes exceptionally hard work and real commitment for believers to defeat him and his schemes.

As Christians, providing we do not faint or give up our fight, we will receive our crown of glory. Fighting against our own will and the devil's schemes is not easy, but with Jesus Christ as our armour, always at our side, we will win as promised by the word of God.

The apostle John said (1 John 4:4): "You, dear children, are from God and have overcome them, because the one in you is greater than the one who is in the world."

I have seen boxers who have been knocked out in the first round, become victorious in the end. Why? Because they did not throw in the towel. I remember one particular heavyweight contest between two great boxing personalities, which attracted enormous attention and big money at the time, but which ended in disaster. To the surprise and disappointment of many, before some of the spectators had even entered the boxing arena, the contest was over. Why? Because one of the protagonists was knocked down within the first few seconds of the start of the fight, and, failing to get up within the allocated time, he was counted out. What a shame! Christians are not like this boxer, however; Christians cannot be counted out, because they can and should get up and fight to the end, they should aim to win the fight.

I have also seen some athletes stumble and fall, but, with the spirit of determination, rise up again to win the race. Rise up to win the race set before you, do not give up or throw in the towel. Fight back and fight hard knowing that you are the best and that you are in the winning team.

Some years ago, in the Champions' League final, Liverpool football team came from 3:0 down in the first half to win 4:3 in the second half: their victory represents one of the greatest miracles in football history, which, for me, shows that all things are possible. I believe that they could not have won had they given up when they were losing 3:0 in the first half, as many other teams would have done. Sometimes it is easy to give up and say it is all over when the going gets tough, when the enemy appears to be firing from all angles and out of all cylinders at you. Paul says that we should proceed into maturity at times like this; this is when we need to summon all our endurance and approach a situation with patience. He tells us:

(2 Timothy 4:7) "I have fought the good fight, I have finished the race, I have kept the faith.

(2 Timothy 4:8) "Now there is in store for me the crown of righteousness, which the Lord, the righteous judge, will, award to me on that day – and not only to me, but also to all who have longed for his appearing."

Background to the Woman of Canaan story as I perceive it

The disciples were fed up with the woman who constantly cried out to Jesus to have mercy on her and help her daughter, and they wanted Jesus to get rid of her.

"Jesus did not answer a word. So his disciples came to him and urged him, 'Send her away, for she keeps crying out after us.' He answered, 'I was sent only to the lost sheep of Israel.' The woman came and knelt before him. 'Lord help me' she said. He replied, 'it is not right to take the children's bread and toss it to their dogs.' 'Yes, Lord.' She said, 'but even the dogs eat the crumbs that fall from their masters' table.' Then Jesus answered, 'Woman, you have great faith! Your request is granted.' And her daughter was healed from that very hour." (Matthew 15:23–28)

The character of the woman in this story is worthy of our emulation. A desperate person, a loving mother who has been knocked down by her daughter's circumstances, she is in need of help. Knowing that Jesus could help her, she held on to her faith; she fought long and hard, and with patience she passed her test of faith, until she received her crown (her daughter was healed).

In today's world, where people want everything instantly and do not even have the patience to wait for an answer to their prayers, how many believers can demonstrate such a great faith in God? In fact, many believers would have failed. We pray, but if we don't receive the answer within the next day or so, we give up and forget about it.

Endurance, fighting long and hard, means that you hold on to your faith in God despite everything that may weaken your resolve.

As a young man, when I made my commitment to follow Christ, I faced all the challenges young people experience. While I was a student at technical school through to when I was at Polytechnic, there were times when I was ridiculed by my friends and classmates because of my Christian lifestyle. I was called many cruel and hurtful names, and to make matters worse, as I did not come from a rich family, life was very difficult for me at times.

Thank God that I did not allow myself to be influenced and nor did I allow myself to be weighed down by any of these challenges. I kept my eyes on Jesus knowing that there were better days ahead of me as prophesised by the Prophet Haggai. I remember particularly one friend who just returned from Nigeria, where he was staying at that time, and he came to advise me. He wanted to teach me how to smoke Indian hemp ("wee" as it was called at that time), which he said would help to enhance my studies. I refused and vehemently declined his offer. Again, I thank God I got through my studies without taking any mind-altering drugs.

There again, in spite of all my financial difficulties, I was always one of the top-performing students in my class. I have never forgotten my time of witnessing about Christ during those difficult times. I remember I went to ask a friend for financial help and he goaded me about my suffering at school, saying that my father must have won the lottery to send me to school. He said that now the lottery money had evaporated this was the reason I was suffering so from financial difficulties. Again, I thank God for all these memories, which are more fulfilling that anything else; because the overriding memory now is that *I did not give up*.

Today, to the glory of God I am counted as one of the workers of God's vineyard and honoured that I am a Pastor, Preacher and Teacher of God's word and an author, broadcaster and radio Evangelist. This is something I would never have dreamed of becoming, ever, in my life. Recently, when I left the United Kingdom to return briefly to Ghana on holiday, I met my friend who had teased me about my financial state all those years ago. He came to me to request financial help, and thank God, I was more than happy to offer him the assistance he needed.

As you read this book, you may also be facing challenges: you may have been knocked out by sickness, suffering because you've lost your job, or be crippled with debt. You may be under intense pressure from your friends, husband or wife, or maybe you are finding it very hard as a student because of your financial circumstances. You might be finding it a challenge to raise your children as a single or unemployed parent, you might be finding it almost impossible, even, but irrespective of your problems, take inspiration from the Woman of Canaan and myself, and hold on to your faith in God.

Fight to the end! Keep calling for the attention of Jesus Christ and you too will receive your reward of a crown. Remember that a race, a fight or football match, is not won until the last whistle. God bless Pastor Matthew of KICC with his words of encouragement: "It is not over until you win!" There is a proverb our Elders in Ghana say, "Don't blame God while it is still day." What they mean by this is that God can turn things around at any time.

While I may not be a Manchester United Football team supporter like my wife, I have great respect for the team because they never give up on a match until the last whistle. Therefore, I never rejoice when the team I support is playing them until the last whistle, even when we are winning, for they have the spirit of fighting to the end. Man-U has won many matches in the last minutes, sometimes even coming back up from behind, when it looked almost impossible.

Many people begin well but lose the crown or the reward because they lack endurance. Many people have lost the race from the beginning, while others persist, coming up from behind to win. I was speaking to a woman recently who wanted to give up; she had even contemplated ending her life because she could not take it anymore. She had been let down by the man she had loved, helped and trusted, and besides this, so much else seemed to have disappointed her. I had so much compassion for her as she told me about her ordeal, but all I could say to her was, "Please, please, do not give up, hold on, for the Lord will see you through."

Paul said that through suffering, believers gain patience, and through patience, experience is achieved. You will have testimony as you patiently win your fight against the devil and situations in life.

(Romans 5:3) "Not only so, but we also rejoice in our sufferings, because we know that suffering produces perseverance ...

(Romans 5:4) "... perseverance, character; and character, hope.

(Romans 5:5) "And hope does not disappoint us, because God has poured out his love into our hearts by the Holy Spirit, whom he has given us."

Finally, with endurance, your sorrow will turn to joy so long as you never give up. Comforting His disciples who were very sad because He was going to die, Jesus said to them, "A woman giving birth to a child has a pain because her time has come; but when her baby is born she forgets the anguish because of her joy that a child is born into the world. So with you: Now is your time of grief, but I will see you again and you will rejoice, and no-one will take away your joy." (John 16:21–22)

Remember the joy of the disciples when the women came with the news that Jesus had risen from death. Consider the joy and relief when Jesus appeared before them in a locked room and said, "Peace be unto you." On your journey to maturity, your grief and your pain will also turn to joy if you hold on to Him as Peter instructed: "And the God of all grace, who called you to his eternal glory in Christ, after you have suffered a little while, will himself restore you and make you strong, firm and steadfast. To him be the power for ever and ever. Amen." (1 Peter 5:10–11)

4. Keeping Fit

(1 Timothy 4:7) "Having nothing to do with godless myths and old wives' tales; rather than train yourself to be godly.

(1 Timothy 4:8) "For physical training is of some value, but godliness has value for all things, holding promise for both the present life and the life to come."

The final part of this section of *Be Ye Transformed* is about how we can mature as Christians, so let us look at how Paul compares the work we need to do to keeping fit. The "plan" this time is to exercise.

Just as physical exercise keeps a person fit and strong, spiritual exercise keeps the mind and spirit healthy. The exercise of godliness is as rigorous and demanding as physical exercise, and makes you feel equally alive. It includes fasting and prayer, reading and meditating. It involves practising the word of God, singing Christian songs for inspiration even at times of suffering, and daily fellowship with other believers to give us strength and stamina. All this, in turn, will help is to stay spiritually fit and defuse any obstacle or hindrances the enemy may try and put in our way to hinder our progress on the way to heaven. It will also help us on our quest to win over others for Christ.

Paul says that in order to stay fit, believers should have nothing to do with "godless myths and old wives' tales"; he counsels us to reject profane and apocryphal fables. What he is saying is this: these believers must move away from manmade traditions and irreligious stories that offer no benefit to one's spiritual fitness, and that we must train ourselves to be godly. Paul is saying that if we want to grow in the things of God, then we must break away from the tenets that represent the commandments of men and not God, just as Jesus told the Pharisees. It is unfortunate that some Christians spend a lot of time watching movies, even horror films, and waste time gossiping rather than reading the Bible or meditating on the word of God. No wonder some Christians have nightmares and other frightening experiences at night.

(Matthew 15:1) "Then some Pharisees and teachers of the law came to Jesus from Jerusalem and asked ...

(Matthew 15:2) "... 'Why do your disciples break the tradition of the elders? They don't wash their hands before they eat!'

(Matthew 15:3) "Jesus replied, 'and why do you break the command of God for the sake of your tradition?'

(Matthew 15:4) "For God said, 'Honour your father and mother' and, 'anyone who curses his father or mother must be put to death.'

(Matthew 15:5) "But you say that if a man says to his father or mother, 'whatever help you might otherwise have received from me is a gift devoted to God ...'

(Matthew 15:6) "... he is not to 'honour his father' with it. Thus you nullify the word of God for the sake of your tradition.

(Matthew 15:7) "You hypocrites! Isaiah was right when he prophesised about you ..."

(Colossians 2:6) "So then, just as you received Christ Jesus as Lord continue to live in him ...

(Colossians 2:7) "... rooted and built up in him, strengthened in the faith as you were taught, and overflowing with thankfulness.

(Colossians 2:8) "See to it that no-one takes you captive through hollow and deceptive philosophy, which depends on human tradition and the basic principles of this world rather than on Christ."

Like the Pharisees, those following the traditions of men are not fit for the kingdom because:

1. The traditions of men break or violate the word of God, because they cause men to disobey the word of God. (Matthew 15:3)
2. The traditions of men render the word of God ineffectual. (Matthew 15:6)
3. The traditions of men reject the word of God. (Mark 7:8–9, 13)

4. The doctrines taught by tradition were the commandments of men not the commandments of God. (Matthew 15:9; Mark 7:6–7)

Brethren, if we want to grow to maturity, that is to be fully transformed as we journey to heaven, we must break away from the traditions of men that nullify the power of the word of God. That is, in refusing to change with the word of God, but instead insisting on holding on to the traditions of humans and the church (i.e. we must always do it this way or that way), and the status quo, you are hindering your own progress. The traditions of men are the enemy of those wishing to grow; they set you back in Christian growth.

Looking back at the circumstances just before the Pharisees, Jesus asked:

"'Why do your disciples break the tradition of the elders? They don't wash their hands before they eat!'" (Matthew 15:2)

Matthew says:

(Matthew 14:35–36) "And when the men of that place recognised Jesus, they sent word to all the surrounding country. People brought all their sick to him and begged him to let the sick just touch the edge of his cloak, and all who touched him were healed."

You can imagine the joy in the city that day. But no matter what was happening, the Pharisees were not totally impressed. All they could do was ask questions about the washing of hands. There is nothing in the Bible that says you must wash your hands before you eat, although there is nothing wrong with that, it is hygienic, but the word of God is the supreme command on which you should act.

Like the Pharisees' arguments those of the traditionalists are not centred on the Bible either, but often refer to the traditions of the Elders or of the church. These people worship men, not God. They are happy to be traditional but not transitional. Tradition will always oppose anything new, irrespective of the benefits.

The main reason that some believers are so tradition-conscious is that they lack the word of God. If we become more word-conscious and concentrate on the word of God, the influence of the traditionalists will diminish and we can grow in the Lord. Believers and churches that hold on to traditions at the expense of paying attention to the word of God, will fail to grow and prosper.

Before concluding Stage Two let me ask you how old you think you are in the Lord. Have there been any changes in your life, or are you still the same? As every parent wants their children to grow, so God desires that

His children grow. A man in Christ is a new creature. Let me remind you of the four rules to enable you to grow in the Lord:

1. Deny yourself of things that will hinder you from growing in the Lord;
2. Put all your efforts and energy into forgetting the past, and press forward to win the race. Give no place to bitterness, past glories and past mistakes, for they will distract you from moving on;
3. Fight long and hard with endurance, and never give up;
4. Keep fit with daily spiritual exercise by fasting, prayer and reading, and practise the word of God.

In this way, one grows to maturity, toward the day when one will meet the Lord face to face.

Again, let me say that as with all the stages, failure to grow or progress to the next stage can result in:

1. Falling away, for there will be trials and temptations. God will test your faith for your own good, but the devil will tempt you to fail; many have fallen at this stage, because they failed to resist the devil's temptations. I am always telling people to beware, for the Devil will con-

stantly try to tempt you. He will look for wherever you are vulnerable; he can detect your weaknesses; he has a good memory for the things you used to do most or liked best when you were in Stage Zero. Knowing that Jesus Christ had fasted for forty days and that therefore he was hungry, the devil went to him with the temptation of food. "If you are the Son of God, tell these stones to become bread." However, Jesus, having been filled with the Spirit, answered, "It is written: 'Man does not live on bread alone, but on every word that comes from the mouth of God." (Matthew 4:3–4)

2. Be warned against becoming stagnant. Do not allow things to become the norm or you will lose your first love – Jesus Christ – and there will be no changes.

Finally, as I end this part of *Be Ye Transformed*, I offer this prayer for myself and for all Ministers of God.

"Dear Lord, make me a doer of your word and let me break away from the traditions of men, but not as a preacher only – as is the habit of other preachers that preach to people while they do things differently – so that after I have preached to others, I myself will not be disqualified for the prize. Amen."

As Paul said (1 Corinthians 9:26), "Therefore I do not run like a man running aimlessly; I do not fight like a man beating the air."

(1 Corinthians 9:27) "No, I beat my body and make it my slave so that after I have preached to others, I myself will not be disqualified for the prize. Amen."

Stage Three: Soul-Winning

Here we are at Stage Three which is about soul-winning – preaching or witnessing to others – a time when every believer, literate or illiterate, is required to share with someone the good news he or she has heard or read. This is the time when every believer, whether young or old in the Lord, is expected to tell others about the gift of salvation that comes through faith in Jesus Christ; that is, to share our faith or the Gospel of Jesus Christ with others. Sharing this knowledge with others is a response to the Great Commission by Jesus Christ, who said to His disciples and all believers:

(Matthew 28:19) "Therefore go and make disciples of all the nations, baptising them in the name of the Father and of the Son and of the Holy Spirit …

(Matthew 28:20) "… and teaching them to obey everything I have commanded you. And surely I am with you always, to the end of the age."

To become a Christian not only marks the end of one's relation with Satan and the material world, but also the beginning of a new life in Christ. You become a servant of Christ, ready to share a new life with others whose aim is also to bring them to Christ. Jesus said:

"You did not choose Me, but I chose you and appointed you that you should go and bear fruit, and *that* your fruit should remain, that whatever you ask the Father in My name He may give you." (John 15:16)

We were all called for a purpose, and that purpose is to go and bear fruit for Christ who saved us. Thus, having a product of the same kind for Christ is one of the reasons why every believer was born into the family of God. Your calling, therefore, is to share what you have in the Lord with someone; in other words, aim to bring them to the Lord.

Jesus says that believers are supposed to bear fruit, but it is unfortunate that most believers bear no fruit and many are unproductive. In the natural realm, it is said that those who fail to have children are barren; in the same way, many believers are barren in the Lord because they fail to bring children of their kind to the Lord. Therefore, if any believer fails to live up to this task of soul winning, s/he has failed in one of their greatest responsibilities to God. For more details on how believers can bear fruit, I recommend that you read my book, *Stay Connected to Christ*, published in 2013.

I believe witnessing or winning souls is not only a command from Jesus, but also a sign of growth in the Lord for every believer. Therefore, if you are reading this book as a believer, a transformed man delivered from the kingdom of darkness into the kingdom of light, and by the grace of God growing in your relationship with God, I would like you to prove your transformation by telling others about the Man, Jesus, behind your new life.

If we as believers want to see people saved and the membership of our churches increase, the answer lies in every believer responding to the great Commission of our Lord: "Go and make disciples of all the nations." However, I know that the big question on many people's lips is this: how long must I be in the Lord before I can start witnessing or telling someone about Christ? While of course I believe that training is important in this matter as in every area of human life, and I certainly have nothing against the notion that people must be well trained in order to be effective in witnessing, I believe also that, whether experienced or inexperienced, there is a simple way to witness and bring people to Christ. Thus, I am totally against the doctrine that disallows people to witness until they have been in training for several years. Witnessing about Christ is not something you must take training or lessons in for years, or pass tests and examinations in before you are qualified to do so; it is not like someone having to pass a driving test before they are allowed to drive.

Some people fail to witness and make excuses such as, "I am not a Pastor, Elder or an Officer of my church"; there are others who insist that, "I am only young in the Lord and I do not know how to witness." To counteract both these excuses, I want you to know that you do not need any qualifications before you can bring people to Christ. In other words, you do not need any qualifications in order to tell someone about your salvation and about He who saved you.

Below, I present you with some simple Bible stories as an easy way by which everybody, young or old in the Lord, can bring people to God regardless of how long they have been with the Lord. It does not matter whether you are male or female, educated or uneducated, an Officer in the church or an ordinary member.

Before I continue, let me give you another reason why many Christians fail to witness: because they have no confidence in God – ministers of God, even – lack confidence in themselves. This is why they find it difficult to witness to others, invite others to God or to the church, all of which would enable them to receive Christ as their Lord and Saviour.

As I have already said, the greatest, the most fundamental job for every Christian, is witnessing or winning souls for Christ. From the stories below, I bring you a simple way by which you can bring people to

Christ, irrespective of your position in the church, educational background, or age in God.

Story One

(2 Kings 5:1–8)

Background

In verse 1, we read that there was a man called Naaman who was a commander of the Aramaic army. Naaman had led the army to many victories although he suffered from leprosy. As to how it was possible that a man with leprosy was able to serve in the army, we are not informed by the Scripture. Leprosy was a serious and disgraceful disease then, as it would be now. In his house was a servant who had been taken captive from Israel.

In Verse 3 it is written, "... one day this girl said [witness about the healing power of God] to her master's wife, 'I wish my master would go to see the prophet in Samaria [which was her home town] who would heal him of his leprosy.'"

In verse 4 Naaman tells the king what the girl had said to him.

In verse 5, the king tells Naaman "By all means go" and says, "I will even give you a letter for the king of Israel". Thus, Naaman sets out with gifts and the letter from the king, which says:

In verse 6, "I present to you my servant Naaman. I want you to heal him of his leprosy."

In verse 7, in contrast, is the stubborn attitude of the King of Israel. The Bible says "... when he read the letter [to me I would say it is out of fear and desperation] he tore his clothes in dismay and said, '... this man has sent me a leper to heal! Am I God that I can kill and give life? He is only trying to find an excuse to invade us again.'"

In verse 8, when Elisha the man of God heard that the king had torn his robes, he sent him this message: "... why have you torn your robes? Let the man come to me and he will know that there is a prophet [God's messenger, God's spokesman, a man who stands in between God and His people] in Israel."

The rest of the story says Naaman, who had set off for Samaria on a horse with ten men and carrying gifts, was told by the prophet to go and bathe seven times in the River Jordan. Naaman became very angry and wanted to go back to Syria, asking "... are there not bigger rivers in Syria than River Jordan?" However, after being persuaded by his aides, he agrees to bathe as ordered by the prophet, and having bathed seven times as he was instructed, he is healed. In fact, the Bible says that not only was he healed, his flesh was restored and became clean again, like that of a young boy. So

Naaman confesses: "Now I know that there is no God in the entire world except in Israel."

Looking at this story and seeing how it relates to how we live today, I ask you this: What do you make of the story now that I have reminded you of how important it is as a believer to win souls for Christ, in Stage Three of your transformation?

And let me ask you another question: What are you doing as a believer?

Coming back to those that say, "Well I am not a Pastor, Elder or an Officer," or "I am too young in the Lord," or "I am illiterate, and I don't know how to witness" I have come to tell all of you, believers – young or old in Christ – that, like Naaman, many people are dying out there. They are perishing, and heading towards hell without Christ. You can make a difference to such people, as we saw with Naaman's life, with your simple invitation to church or to Christ, He who is the way to eternal life.

We read in verse 3 the simple word (witnessing) of a captive servant girl, a stranger in a foreign land, serving her mistress, who testifies to the healing power of God in her land of Israel. These simple words brought healing and faith to a powerful Aramaic captain. The action of this poor, unknown girl shows the confidence she had in what the Lord can do through his prophet:

your faith and simple words will do the same. They will bring salvation and faith to someone.

As I said earlier in my introduction to this story, many believers, unlike the girl in Naaman's story, fail to tell (witness) others about God. This may be because of their lack of faith in God; their lack of confidence in the ministers of God – and it may even be due to a lack of confidence in themselves – but I also believe that they fail to adhere to the advice King Jehoshaphat gave to Israel; advice that I believe was meant for all believers:

"Early in the morning they left for the Dessert of Tekoa. As they set out, Jehoshaphat stood and said, 'Listen to me, Judah and people of Jerusalem! Have faith in the Lord your God and you will be upheld; have faith in his prophets and you shall be successful.'" (2 Chronicles 20:20)

What it means is this: if you have faith in God, He will provide you with moral support and inspire you with any confidence you lack in order to do anything you propose to do in life, and this is true even at times of willingness to witness in the context of Stage Three of this book.

If you have faith in the prophets of God, you will be successful in anything you do. I repeat: when you follow or obey the instructions offered by the prophets of God, you will be successful in all that you do. Have faith in God and He will provide for you and defend you, maintain you to attain whatever you need, or to face any hostilities in life.

Brethren; no matter whether your position is high or low, your age in God young or old, you are of use to spread the word of the Gospel of the Lord, in order that you bring salvation to someone. Just look for the opportunity and avail yourself to tell others what the Lord can do for the lives of His people, just as Peter and the eleven disciples did when they took advantage of a public event on the day of Pentecost to present the Gospel to 3,000 souls, bringing them to Christ. (Acts 2:41)

In just the same way, God presents to His children opportunities to spread the Good News to others who may need it and to all those who are sensitive to the Holy Spirit. Take the lead with bold steps and present Christ to the dying world and God will bless you.

In verse 7 of 2 Kings, chapter 5, unlike the servant girl we have just discussed who had so much confidence in what the Lord can do through the prophet, the King of Israel, who after all is supposed to know more than the girl about what the Lord can do through the prophet, became very angry and fearful. Out of desperation, he tore his robes and said, "Am I God? Can I kill and bring back to life?" Do you realise that the action of the king could have made Naaman turn away from God and loose his healing?

The action of the king, to me, is like those believers who are supposed to know what the Lord can do, but fail to witness to this dying world. Worst of all, in my view, are those who not only fail to bring people to the Lord, but also drive people away from God, seemingly forgetting what Jesus said. Matthew (18:6) illustrates this point: "But if anyone causes one of these little ones who believe in me to sin, it would be better for him to have a large millstone hung around his neck and to be drowned in the depths of the sea."

What am I saying here? I am stating that if you fail to bring souls to God that is one thing, but be very careful indeed not to turn anyone away as it is a very dangerous act, which offends God according to Jesus. As a leader of a church, I have seen many people leave, not because they don't like the church, but for other reasons that relate to the leader and other things. Many people often presume that they have been offended by someone else in the church, and an instance of this is when people begin to gossip about others.

I was once told a story about a woman who joined a certain church and became a very committed member but, unfortunately, this woman stopped going to the church. The Pastor kept ringing her to ask why she was not attending church any more. She would always tell the Pastor that she was busy. After several attempts, the Pastor realised that she had made up her mind not to come, and so he gave up his chase. Later on, I was told that the Pastor was informed about why the woman had stopped attending; it was because the services at the church were held in the afternoon, and as she worked in the morning, she felt that she could only attend church in her work clothes after she had finished work. Apparently, there had been someone in the church that was more preoccupied with what people wore to church than with the word of God and, allegedly, this person had gossiped about the way the woman dressed. When the woman had heard that her dress sense was being gossiped about, she had decided to stop going to church. Unfortunately, this woman's situation is just one of many similar incidences where people are driven out of church and from the presence of God. This is a very sad state of affairs.

The worst part about all of this is that, often, the very people responsible for turning people away are the same people that complain and blame the leader or leaders about lack of growth in the church. Let me give you some advice: it is better to bring people to Christ to be blessed than it is to turn people away from Him, which will attract curses. Therefore, I urge you to be vigilant of the actions and attitudes you project in church.

In verse 8 of 2 Kings, chapter 5, like the servant girl, the prophet, who knows what the Lord can do through him, declared boldly: "... let him come," and when he [Naaman] had come, the Lord healed him through simple instruction from the Prophet, the Man of God, but not until the poor girl had directed him.

What do you know about the God who has saved you through our Lord and Saviour Jesus Christ? To whom have you witnessed since He saved you?

Unlike the girl directing Naaman to the prophet, we can ourselves preach the Gospel and witness about Christ who was sent to save all men from their sins. Let me remind you, you are not God who can save or bring deliverance to people, but you can direct them to Him so that He can. Do not act like the king, therefore, who nearly turned away a man who needed help. Do not be like those who gossip about what people wear, or those who chatter about what others do in church, for these actions have a tendency to turn people away.

There is good news: Naaman was healed and his flesh was restored. God gave him a new body; he became clean again with skin like that of a young boy. Your confidence in God, and your compassion for others, can and will produce the same for someone else; someone will be reborn; will become new as the result of your witnessing, your testimony, or through your invitation.

In concluding this story, let me say one thing: if you are reading this book as a non-believer at Stage Zero, then like the servant girl in Naaman's story, I invite you to come to Christ who saved me and is prepared to save you too. You may have everything you thought you ever needed in this world, but like Naaman, I want you to know that you are sick. You suffer a very shameful disease even more serious than leprosy, because you are without Christ. You are heading towards hell, because as Jesus said, "What good is it for a man to gain the whole world, yet forfeit his soul? Or what can a man give in exchange for his soul?" (Mark 8:36–37)

If you come to Christ now, He will save you: "Come to Jesus and you will be saved, for salvation is found in no-one else, for there is no other name under heaven given to men by which we must be saved." (Acts 4:12)

Story Two:
This second story, which is in Mark 2:1-5, speaks about Jesus forgiving and healing a paralysed man. In this story we are introduced to four men who express their faith in Jesus Christ in a profound way. I think their level of faith sets an example for all believers. The story starts with Jesus preaching the word in a house in Capernaum. A large number of people gathered around him to hear him speak. There was nowhere left to stand or sit in that house so the crowd poured out onto the areas outside. The story goes on to tell us that these four men had a friend or a relative who was paralyzed. They took him along to Capernaum simply with the expec-

tation that Jesus would heal him. They got there and found the large crowd gathered outside the house Jesus was preaching in. They could not get through the crowd to see Jesus. Imagine carrying a paralysed man over a long journey to a physician only to get there to find the physician inaccessible. What would you do? Since they could not get through the crowd to see Jesus, they made an opening in the roof and lowered the man on a mat - a stretcher like device - to Jesus. I cannot tell you why these four men took such a risk, but without doubt it demonstrates their eagerness to get the paralyzed man healed. The story concludes that when Jesus saw the faith of the four men, he said to the paralyzed man, *"son, your sins are forgiven....arise, take up your bed and go to your house"*. The man was immediately healed and his sins were forgiven.

I hope you noticed something very significant in the story. The bible says that when Jesus saw the faith of the four men, he said to the paralyzed man, *"son, your sins are forgiven"*. Now I believe that the same principle applies today as it did all those years ago. Your faith in Jesus Christ and his abilities can bring healing, forgiveness of sins and even salvation to someone else. The bible continues this story with Jesus saying to the paralytic, *"arise, take up your bed, and go to your house"*. We learn that the faith of the four men produced results because the paralytic man immediately stood up, took his bed, and walked out. He did as he was commanded in full view of everyone. All were amazed and glorified God, saying, *"we never saw anything like this"*. From this story I also believe that your faith in Jesus can act as a powerful force to bring others to Christ. I say this because you generally cannot introduce people to strangers. If you do not know or believe in Jesus than I can confidently tell you that you will struggle to introduce people to Him. The Apostle Paul in a letter to the Roman church, again centuries ago, qualified this view by saying *"but how are people to call upon Him whom they have not believed [in whom they have no faith, on whom they have no reliance]?"* (Amplified Bible - Romans 10:14).

As I said earlier many believers fail to bring the unsaved and the needy to Christ. I believe this is because they lack faith in God and in themselves. The four men demonstrated their faith in Jesus through their action. James 2:26 reminds us that *"faith without works is dead"*. The four men believed that Jesus could heal the paralytic man and therefore acted on their belief and used all available means to get him to Jesus. They risked everything. They took the opportunity of Jesus' presence in Capernaum to get the paralyzed man healed. The good news is that after they did their part, Jesus did the rest by giving them the miracle they were hoping for. Fellow believers what I want you to know from this story is that there are so many physically, emotionally and psychologically disabled men and women out there who cannot for one reason or another get to Jesus Christ to access salvation and healing. I use the term disabled here colloquially to mean unbelievers. Remember that in earlier parts of this book; stage zero, I discussed that the unsaved man was weak and unable to save himself from his condition and therefore needed assistance to get out of his nature to salvation. Now I want you to be honest with yourself. Since becoming a Christian, have you introduced any unbelievers to Christ? Is there anyone in the body of Christ that you can say you brought to Jesus? If there isn't then I want to tell you quite bluntly that time is running out.

Day in and day out the Lord presents us with opportunities to tell people about Him, to bring the unsaved into the fold and unto a path of salvation. Seize each of these opportunities to do just that. Take for-instance what Peter and the other eleven disciples did on the day of Pentecost. Paraphrasing from Acts 2: 4-7, 14 and 41, they - that is those who had gathered in the room to pray - were filled with the Holy Spirit and began to speak in other tongues as the Spirit enabled them. When Jerusalem's God-fearing Jews from every nation under heaven heard this sound, a crowd came together in bewilderment, because each person heard their own native tongue being spoken. Utterly amazed, they asked; *"aren't all these who are speaking Galileans?"* They were probably thinking to themselves how is this possible. Peter seized the opportunity, stood up with the eleven, and addressed the crowd to explain about the author of the phenomenon - Jesus Christ. Firstly those who accepted Peter's message were baptized. Secondly about three thousand were added to their number (which is the body of Christ) that day. Now that is what I call an amazing result. If you are not seizing opportunities to introduce people to Jesus, my prayer for you is that the Holy Spirit emboldens you to do so from this day. Take a risk. Who knows; you may win twice as many souls into the kingdom.

Now the flip side of the coin is people who knowingly or unknowingly, cause others to leave the Kingdom of God. People who seize opportunities to rather discourage Christians from obeying God or worse still, to chase them out of the kingdom. Let us go back to my earlier story and take for-instance the crowd outside the house in Capernaum where Jesus was preaching. Did they intentionally prevent the four men from more easily accessing Jesus? Were they perhaps outside the house with an eagerness to see and hear Jesus and therefore naturally blocking the entrance to the house? Were they in their eagerness to hear and see Jesus deaf to the plight of the paralyzed man and the four men trying desperately to get through to see Jesus? I believe their intention or attitude would have encouraged or prevented others from persevering to see or hear Jesus. Likewise, your attitude in or outside the church, about your church, other members thereof or even the Pastor can either attract people to Christ and to your church or, have the opposite effect. Do not underestimate this. Jesus said to his disciples *"Things that cause people to stumble are bound to come, but woe to anyone through whom they come. It would be better for them to be thrown into the sea with a millstone tied around their neck than to cause one of these little ones to stumble"* (Luke 17:1-2). Accidents and misunderstandings will come, but do not discourage and deter people from entering the kingdom of God. I will expand further and also say that never be a hindrance to someone else's pursuit of salvation. Why don't you do your best to be the one through whom others get to know Christ. I guarantee you that you will be blessed. In his prophecy about the end time Daniel said that *"those who lead many to righteousness will shine like the stars for ever and ever"* (Daniel 12:3). I want to encourage you to do what you can, wherever and whenever you can, to introduce people to Christ. Is your intention or your attitude in and outside the church enticing people to Christ or it is driving people out from him? Think about this.

Story Three

(John 43:51) Philip invites Nathanael to Christ

"The next day Jesus decided to leave for Galilee. Finding Philip, he said to him, 'Follow me.' Philip, like Andrew and Peter, was from the town of Bethsaida. Philip found Nathanael and told him, 'We have found the one Moses wrote about in the Law, and about whom the prophets also wrote – Jesus of Nazareth, the son of Joseph.'

'Nazareth! Can anything good come from there?' Nathanael asked.

'Come and see,' said Philip.

When Jesus saw Nathanael approaching, He said of him, 'Here is a true Israelite, in whom there is nothing false.'

'How do you know me?' Nathanael asked.

Jesus answered, 'I saw you while you were still under the fig-tree before Philip called you.'

Then Nathanael declared, 'Rabbi, you are the Son of God! You are the King of Israel.'

Jesus said, 'You believe because I told you I saw you under the fig-tree. You shall see greater things than that.' He then added, 'I tell you the truth, you shall see heaven open, and the angels of God ascending and descending on the Son of Man.'"

I assume that Philip was probably only a few minutes or a few hours old in the Lord (meeting and receiving Christ) when he brought Nathanael to Christ. Philip could not keep the good news to himself, so he called his friend who also came to receive Christ.

Notice the few words from Philip, "'We have found the one Moses wrote about in the Law, and about whom the prophets also wrote – Jesus of Nazareth – the son of Joseph.'

'Nazareth! Can anything good come from there?' Nathanael asked.

'Come and see,' said Philip."

When Nathanael appears to doubt Jesus, Philip invites him "to come and see". Thank God that when Nathanael goes to meet Jesus, he sees that He is truly who Philip says He is.

You see how another simple word can bring salvation to somebody. However, there is another word of warning here, because something I know is this: sometimes someone can respond to your invitation to come to church with the sole aim of seeing what is going on in your church. Furthermore, sometimes, someone will respond to your invitation just to please you; but irrespective of his or her hidden agenda, Jesus has the power to influence everybody that comes to Him.

Let me give you an example. Recently a girl invited her brother into our church and, thank God, that day the message was so powerful, encouraging, challenging and full of conviction that at the end of the service he gave his life to Christ. When he was welcomed into the church, he said, "I came here today just to please my sister who invited me, even when I was sitting down my mind was fixed on when I could leave here. I was thinking that I would not come back any more, but as the preaching went on, I had to change my mind and I wanted to receive Christ as Lord and Saviour." I led him to Christ and prayed for him and, thank God, he has been coming to my services ever since. You can do the same. Don't deny your brothers, sisters and friends, anyone, the grace of Christ for salvation.

Story Four
(John 4: *Jesus Talks With a Samaritan Woman*)

In Verse 4, it says that Jesus had to go through Samaria *en route* to Galilee, but do you know why? Because He was about to break a barrier, and the barrier He was about to break was a traditional one between the Jews and the Samaritans. However, most pertinently for me in the context of this book, is this: He had to go through Samaria because of a woman who would soon be an evangelist: a soul-winning vessel.

Jesus is our role model, by which we should respect all people. Through Him we learn that all people – whether black or white – people of all races, can meet together to worship God.

In verse 28–30 we are told that the Samaritan woman then left her water jar and went back to the town, and that once there, she said to the people, "Come, see a man who told me everything I ever did. Could this be the Christ?" Then they went out of the town and went to meet Him. Just as Philip could not keep the good news about the Messiah to himself and called Nathanael, so the Samaritan woman could not deny her people of the knowledge of Jesus, even though she had little experience or training. The Bible says she **left her water jar**, went to the town and began to witness within only a few minutes of meeting Jesus, with these simple words she told them: **"Come, see a man who told me everything I ever did …"**

God bless my best friend and co-worker in Christ's vineyard, Pastor Godfred Peter Obeng General Overseer, Harvestime Ministries International! He once preached: "Jesus asked the Samaritan woman for only a cup of water, which she refused to give him because he was a Jew, but when she realised who Jesus was – the Son of God – she gave Him the whole jar full of water. This woman's action towards Jesus means that if you really see who Jesus is as the woman did, and then you will give Him all that you have. Do you think you have given Him all that you have since you found Him? Alternatively, like most people, have you only given Him part of what you have? Let me remind you once again that Christianity requires full surrender to Christ our Lord."

The result of the Samaritan Woman's testimony In verse 39–42, we learn that: "Many of the Samaritans from that town believed in him because of the woman's testimony, 'He told me everything I ever did.' So when the Samaritans came to him they urged him to stay with them, and he stayed two days. And because of his words many more became believers. They said to the woman, 'we no longer believe just because of what you said; now we have heard for ourselves, and we know that this man really is the Saviour of the world.'" Jesus will always prove himself to anyone who comes to Him. Men may let you down. I have seen and heard of people who have been seriously let down by those they'd helped, introducing them into jobs or relationships, but I can assure you that you will never ever be disappointed if you introduce someone to Christ.

Like Philip and Nathanael, Jesus took over from the woman, and the Bible says many believed as a result.

I don't know what message you are getting from these three stories, but for me, they say a lot about bringing people to Christ in a most simple and direct way.

Let me ask you the following questions:

How long have you been a Christian, or how long is it since you first met Christ? What did you see in Jesus when you first met Him and who do you think He is? What do you say about Him? The Samaritan woman, for example, asked, "Could He be the Christ?" While the other Samaritans said, "We know that this man really is the Saviour of the world."

What is your reaction to the questions above; do you want to see people saved? Do you want to see churches full of souls?

If your answer is "Yes", then begin to invite people to the Lord and into your church.

Yes! You may not be a Pastor or an Elder, and you may even be very young in the Lord, but your invitation can and will make a great difference to somebody's life. Jesus through His Pastors, men and women of God, will speak to them when they come.

Take the story of Luke (16:19–31), but especially 27–31 (the rich man and poor Lazarus):

(Luke 16:27) "He answered, 'Then I beg you, father, send Lazarus to my father's house …'

(Luke 16:28) '… for I have five brothers. Let him warn them, so that they will not also come to this place of torment.'

(Luke 16:29) Abraham replied, 'They have Moses and the Prophets; let them listen to them.'

(Luke 16:30) 'No, father Abraham,' he said, 'but if someone from the dead goes to them, they will repent.'

(Luke 16:31) He said to him, 'if they do listen to Moses and the Prophets, they will not be convinced even if someone rises from the dead.'"

How old are you in the Lord? How many people have you invited or brought to Christ since you met Him? How many have followed you to your church since you became a member? Even the rich dead man wanted the Gospel to be preached to his fathers' household, unfortunately for him, though, it was too late, because there is no repentance for a dead person. Do not wait until you are dead before you become an evangelist, because it will be too late for you too. Do it now and see the result before you die.

Before I end Stage Three, allow me ask you some important questions:

What are you doing now as a believer?

How do you think about others who are not born again?

Have you had the time to think about where non-believers will be going when they die?

Do you want to see many people saved into the kingdom of God?

Do you want to see your church grow?

If your answers to all these questions resounds "Yes", then I challenge you to act now. Go then and invite people, God has men and women ready to preach to them. Do not make excuses by saying, "I can't" for God only needs your desire. Step out in faith and He will help you through with His Spirit. You can do it, for your competency comes from God, just as Paul said.

The Evangelist Reinhard Bonke says that he wants to see heaven full and hell empty, thus to that end he never stops evangelising. It does not matter how old you are in the church. It only took a few words from an unknown servant girl in a foreign land to testify about the healing power of God. Those few words brought healing to one of the most powerful men on earth at the time. Philip, I presume, was only a few minutes old when he brought Nathanael to salvation. The Samaritan woman was seemingly so unworthy, yet within a few minutes of meeting the Master, she brought the whole community to Christ. Do not wait until you die before you come to know the importance of soul-winning or bringing people to Christ; do not be like the rich man. Do not leave it too late if you would like to assist in evangelistic work. Be obedient to the command of the Master: "Go and be a disciple of all nations".

I want to encourage you by saying that everything you acquire here on earth will be left behind when you die. As Job said in Job 1:21, "Naked I came from my mother's womb, and naked I shall depart." Praise God that the only things that will accompany you to heaven are the souls you win for Christ. Daniel (12:3) says that those who turn many to righteousness will shine like stars, for ever and ever. All it takes is your invitation if you have no experience to preach, so do something today. Is there anybody you know who is ready to say, "God, here am I, Lord use me"? God bless you as you respond to the Great Commission for there is a great reward in soul-winning. As you read this book, let me ask you another question: if you pass on to heaven now who will accompany you before God? Will you be accompanied by any souls you have won for Christ?

If someone needs your help to come to know the Master, please do not deny this person the opportunity. Paul said, "'Everyone who calls on the name of the Lord will be saved.' How, then, can they call on the one they have not believed in? And how can they believe in the one of whom they have not heard? And how can they hear without someone preaching to them? And how can they preach unless they are sent? As it is written, 'how beautiful are the feet of those who bring good news!'" (Romans 10:13–15)

The quotation above is a clear indication that there are people everywhere who may not know who Jesus is or know about His great work, that He died on the cross to save mankind from his sins. They will only know, believe, or be saved through their faith. They will find faith after they are told about Jesus and then grow in faith when they are nurtured in His name. So do your part by availing yourself to the Lord. Let Him use you to bring repentance to someone, and God will reward you, as Daniel tells us.

Believers will be held responsible for failing to witness because we are all indebted to God for saving us, and therefore, it is our responsibility to pay Him back by introducing others to Him too. The Bible says He does not want anyone to perish. According to the Prophet Ezekiel, believers will be judged for failing to witness, so do not think you can just sit back happy and comfortable because you have been saved:

"When I say to a wicked man, 'You will surely die,' and you do not warn him or speak out to dissuade him from his evil ways in order to save his life, that wicked man will die for his sin, and I will hold you accountable for his blood. But if you do warn the wicked man and he does not turn from his wickedness or from his evil ways, he will die for his sin; but you will have saved yourself." (Ezekiel 3:18–19)

And here is Ezekiel again:

"But if the watchman sees the sword coming and does not blow the trumpet to warn the people and the sword comes and takes the life of one of them, that man will be taken away because of his sin, but I will hold the watchman accountable for his blood. Son of Man, I have made you a watchman for the house of Israel; so hear the word I speak and give them warning from me. When I say to the wicked, 'O wicked man, you will surely die,' and you do not speak out to dissuade him from his ways, that wicked man will die for his sin, and I will hold you accountable for his blood. But if you do warn the wicked man to turn from his ways and he does not do so, he will die for his sin, but you will be saved yourself." (Ezekiel 33:6–9)

I was once witnessing about Christ to a former work colleague who said to me, "My friend, do you know why I don't believe in Christ and your Christianity?"

"No," I said, "please tell me."

"Every good thing in this world is preserved and kept secret and hidden from other people," he said. "Christians go round telling everybody about the so-called Christ, inviting everyone to become a Christian, claiming it is the right way. However, when a person discovers something so precious, surely she or he will want to keep it to him or herself, and omit to tell others. That is why I don't believe in your Christ and Christianity as something precious."

Now, what this man and many others do not realise is this, Jesus and Christianity are unique, which is a fact all those who believe never question. Even though my former colleague did not believe what Christians were telling everyone, I on the other hand, was doing my part by responding to the Great Commission.

Now let me move on to discuss the Fourth and the Final Stage – the Ultimate Stage – but before I do so, I thank God for your desire to share your faith with others, and invite them to Christ. I pray that the Spirit of God will give you utterance and boldness as you begin to witness.

Let me remind you of what Paul said to Philemon, "I pray that you may be active in sharing your faith, so that you will have a full understanding of every good thing we have in Christ." (Philemon 1:6)

Stage Four: The Ultimate Stage

This final phase is called the Ultimate Stage. This is because it is the most significant stage in the process of your transformation. It is also the crucial turning point in every believer's life, as I have experienced and witnessed. Due to the importance if this stage in every believer's life, I affirm in my prayers and desires that every believer, young or old, will progress to Stage Four, the Ultimate Stage where the believer will be fully transformed and Christianity will enhance and change your life in addition to strengthening your relationship with God. When you reach the Ultimate Stage, Christianity will become the most important force in your life rather than being mere "religion". Those who fail to reach this stage view Christianity simply as a "religion" and fail to reach this level, which defines your spiritual connection with God at the highest.

Here are the practical realities of reaching the Ultimate Stage: one has to progress through all the previous stages: from the bottom, beginning with that of the non-believer (Stage Zero). Then one must rise to the Stage of Repentance (Stage One). One must then work up to the Stage of Christian Growth (Stage Two), and then practise the level of soul-winning, where one will preach or witness to others, but the goal of which is to win souls for Christ (Stage Three). When the believer is mature, when he has learned and listened, when he believes and meditates on the word of God, then he is putting into practise everything he has learned. Now he is a true believer; he has reached the Ultimate Stage in his relationship with God. Now the believer has been fully transformed.

In response to this, James counsels his readers: "Do not merely listen to the word, and so deceive you. Do what it says." (James 1:22)

At this point, the believer's life reflects what he believes and, therefore, he practices what he preaches. He is fully persuaded and totally committed to following God; and he does what the word of God says, irrespective of the circumstances. Like James, now, the believer sees that what the word of God says is final.

Despite all the benefits the Ultimate Stage offers, it fills me with sadness to see that so many believers never reach this level, and it is interesting, really, when you consider that once you get to this stage, all the other stages appear so easy. At the Ultimate Stage, life becomes, as someone put it, "like living in heaven on earth". At this stage, God becomes more real; He is closer to you as a believer.

The Bible makes it clear that those who have progressed to the Ultimate Stage have come to know that it is not enough only to believe; it is not enough, even, simply to preach the word of God. You must also follow and apply the word of God to your daily activities and decisions.

While many believers are guaranteed a place in heaven, they nonetheless struggle to receive assurance from God. Why is that? For the simple reason that while they may read and listen to the word of God they have failed to put His word into practise in life.

Ezra is a fitting example for all those who aspire to reach the Ultimate Stage of Christian life before or after reading this book. Ezra did not only study and preach the word as many believers do, but also put it into practise. Like Ezra, we should be determined in both our study and obedience to God's word. For Ezra, the word delivered whatever it said it would. Ezra had prepared his heart to seek the Law of the Lord and to live it, and to teach statutes and ordinances in Israel. (Ezra 7:10)

In fact, as I said earlier on, it becomes easier and more comfortable for a believer to teach others what he has learned or heard when he has begun to live by or practise what he has learned. For example, after I had passed my driving test I began to feel comfortable and self-assured enough to help someone else that wanted to learn to drive. Similarly, teachers are qualified to teach because they have practised something taught to them by someone else. Take, for example, someone who has put into practise any principle from the Bible, such as that of giving generously, and has then seen the result. He or she will be much happier to teach others as well once they have learned and then experienced the concept of giving generously as taught by the Bible.

In addition, as I said earlier, those who progress to the Ultimate Stage, by the grace of God, have reached a turning point in their life. From now on all their focus and all their actions will be based on the word of God, and nothing else. At this wonderful stage, believers are controlled by the Spirit, as advised by Paul, and they no longer have anything to do with the work of the flesh, which encompass the five bodily senses.

Paul said (Galatians 5:16) "So I say, live by the Spirit, and you will not gratify the desires of the sinful nature.

(Galatians 5:17) "For the sinful nature desires what is contrary to the Spirit and the Spirit what is contrary to the sinful nature. They are in conflict with each other, so that you do not do what you want.

(Galatians 5:18) "But if you are led by the Spirit, you are not under law."

Those who live by the Spirit have decided to live according to God's word, irrespective of what others say or think, and do not even respond to what their own body tells them. That is to say, they live by faith and not by sight.

The five bodily senses, which are also of the flesh, are:

1. The eyes to see
2. The ears to hear
3. The nose to smell
4. The tongue to taste
5. The nerves to touch

The following directives on the bodily senses are found in (Galatians 5:19–21):

(Galatians 5:19) "The acts of the sinful nature are obvious: sexual immorality, impurity and debauchery …

(Galatians 5:20) "… idolatry and witchcraft; hatred, discord, jealousy, fits of rage, selfish ambition, dissension, factions …

(Galatians 5:21) "… envy, drunkenness, orgies, and the like. I warn you as I did before, that those who live like this will not inherit the kingdom of God."

The works of the Spirit are:

(Galatians 5:22) "But the fruit of the Spirit is love, joy, peace, patience, kindness, goodness, faithfulness …

(Galatians 5:23) "… gentleness and self-control. Against such things there is no law."

(Galatians 5:24) "Those who belong to Christ Jesus have crucified the sinful nature with its passions and desires."

Paul says, "For we live by faith not by sight." (2 Corinthians 5:7) that is, those who have progressed to what I call the Ultimate Stage pay no attention to the flesh, what they see, hear, smell, or taste; they ignore what they feel, and instead are led or controlled by the Spirit. No one can walk with God while he is under the control of the flesh, because God does not work through our flesh, but through our spirit.

Like Abraham, true believers – and for that matter those who have progressed to Stage Four – are fully confident that, irrespective of what happens, God will bring to pass whatever He has said He will do. These people, therefore, have total confidence in God's word, and have the patience to wait for whatever they have asked of God in prayer, no matter how long it takes.

It is true that believers at this stage have also renewed their minds and, as a result, even their confessions have changed. Negative confessions become something of the past, because the word gives way to a positive mind-set that leaves no room for sadness, negative thoughts or negative confessions.

The word allows us to alter our perceptions; lets us see things from God's perspective no matter what the majority see, what they say or how bad the situation may appear. Like Joshua and Caleb who stuck to their belief when Israel was in the wilderness, even though the majority said, "We cannot take the land", because they were afraid of the people there, Joshua and Caleb said, "We can take it". Why? Because Joshua and Caleb believed in God and what He had said, which was, "I have given you the Land". The result of their faith in God against the majority decision, as the Scripture records, was that they were the only two adults to experience Egyptian slavery and live to enter the Promised Land.

Everyone who has reached the Ultimate Stage has done so because – as I said earlier – she or he is controlled by the Spirit. They do whatever God demands of them, never making a decision without taking into consideration what the word of God says about the situation. They judge every situation by the word of God, irrespective of the circumstances. These people never act on what others are doing, or listen to what others are saying, but listen only to what God is saying through His word. Those who fail to progress to the Ultimate Stage are controlled by the flesh because they always want to see, hear, taste, smell and touch before they act.

Knowing what the word of God says, those at the Ultimate Stage are certain of two things: not only are they saved and thus guaranteed a place in heaven, but also, here on earth, they are guaranteed prosperity and success.

According to the word of God, after the death of Moses, the Lord commanded Joshua to lead the Israelites to the promised Land, and said to him: ***"Do not let this Book of the Law depart from your mouth; meditate on it day and night, so that you may be careful to do everything written in it. Then you will be prosperous and successful." (Joshua 1:8)***

Moses, the servant of God and the leader of the Israelites, had died; Joshua was his assistant and was appointed to succeed Moses before his death through the support of God (Numbers 27:15–23; Deuteronomy 3:28). Joshua was then appointed to take the people to the Promised Land. What a big task that is for such a young man to continue a job started by such a remarkable and dedicated leader, a person so close to God, and committed to his duty.

This is yet more proof as to the importance of the Ultimate Stage. As one who has reached the Ultimate Stage, the Scriptures record that Joshua followed all the directives that the Lord gave him so that he prospered and succeeded in everything he did. (Joshua 11–12; 1–24)

- He defeated six nations and thirty-one kings.
- He was one of only two adults in his generation who experienced Egyptian slavery and lived to enter the Promised Land, as I said earlier on.
- He led the Israelites to the Promised Land, their God-given homeland, successfully, and having subdued the Canaanites, he divided the land for the people as he was commanded by God, having first managed to lead them across the River Jordan on dry land.
- He demonstrated his commitment to God before his people, when he said:
- "But if serving the Lord seems undesirable to you, then choose for yourselves this day who you will serve, whether the gods your forefathers served beyond the River, or the gods of the Amorites, in whose land you are living. But as for me and my household, we will serve the Lord" (Joshua 24:15).
- Joshua, like many others at this stage, will insist: "No matter which God you chose to serve, I have already made up my mind to obey and serve the one and only true God Jesus Christ.

We all want to be successful and prosperous in life, but from Joshua's successful story, I would like to say that Joshua 1:8 is the key direction that we all must follow, so allow me to advise you, that if you want success in every area of your life, follow the method the Lord gave, which is:

- First, never allow the book of the Law (the word of God) to depart from your mouth. That is to say, keep reading, studying or listening to the word of God, keep feeding your spirit with it at all times.

- Secondly, always meditate on or keep thinking about what you have read or heard. To meditate in this context in the original Hebrew is "*hagar*", which means to ponder, roar, imagine, murmur, mutter, speak, talk or utter. This means that to meditate is much more than thinking about the word; it is to voice aloud as you think about it, speaking or talking to yourself about the word you read.

- Finally always put into practise what you have read or learnt and therefore what you meditating on, and as the Lord promised Joshua, and in the context of this book, you too will attain the Ultimate Stage, and prosper and succeed in everything you do.

In the form of an equation, you can put it thus: Reading/studying/listening to the word of God + Meditating + Practicing = Success and Prosperity.

Many people are not successful in life because, even though they may be Christians, yet they do not take the reading of the Scriptures seriously. There are others too, who will read or listen to the Scriptures, but will not meditate on them. Finally, some people will read and meditate on the Scriptures, but fail to put God's word into practice. It is better to know that the only way to achieve success and prosperity is to do all the three

Again, like Abraham the father of faith and an example of a true believer, all those who reach the Ultimate Stage in the context of this book, have absolute faith in God. They know that whatever the Lord has said will always come to pass for them, that is, it will be so. The Bible says that when God called him to (Abraham) and ordered him to leave his people and his father's house and go to where He the Lord would show him, he had enough confidence in God, so much in fact that he set fourth even though he did not know where he was going. This is because Abraham was fully persuaded that he would not be disappointed by God's promise, so he was also giving glory to God (Genesis 12). This is the nature and the attitude of those who are at the Ultimate Stage; they are always joyful, giving glory and thanks to God at all times, and in every situation.

If you have set your heart on doing something because you believe the Lord has told you to do it, then I encourage you to keep it up. Never give up, but continue to give glory to God no matter how discouraging it may look. God always fulfils what He has said He will do. He blessed Abraham as result of his obedience and He will do the same for you; this is the comfort of those at the Ultimate Stage.

In recommending Abraham's action, Paul has this to say in a letter to the Romans' Church:

"Without weakening in his faith, he faced the fact that his body was as good as dead – since he was about a hundred years old – and that Sarah's womb was also dead. Yet he did not waver through unbelief regarding the promise of God, but strengthened in his faith and gave glory to God. Being fully persuaded that God had power to do what he had promised." (Romans 4:19–21)

Many believers fail to progress to the Ultimate Stage because they fail to submit to the will and the purpose of God, even though they may faithfully go to church.

Another example of Abraham's faith in God is his obedience and readiness to sacrifice his son, Isaac, at the request of the Lord. The Bible tells us that Abraham had total confidence in God's provision:

"Isaac spoke up and said to his Father Abraham, 'Father?'

'Yes, my son?' Abraham replied.

'The fire and wood are here,' Isaac said, 'But where is the lamb for the burnt offering?'

Abraham answered, 'God himself will provide the lamb for the burnt offering, my son.' And the two of them went on together." (Genesis 22:7–8)

The author of Hebrews relates that:

By faith, Abraham, when he was tested, offered up Isaac, and he who had received the promises offered up his only begotten *son*, of whom it was said, *'In Isaac your seed shall be called'*, concluding that God *was* able to raise *him* up, even from the dead, from which He also received him in a figurative sense. (Hebrews 11:17–19)

Unlike Abraham, most people, and even, to an extent, believers, will only be ready to give to the Lord and give to others, when they have more to spare, and these people are governed by the laws of the world more than the laws of God. For the Akan's from Ghana there is a proverb about this idea of giving only when you have more, it says "You don't give up your only child to live with somebody." This is something many Ghanaians do; it is part of the country's tradition, but what this proverb means is that you only give up your child if you have more than one child, so that after you have given one away you still have another one left to live with. What I am saying is this: the person at the Ultimate Stage will give out his child even if it is his only one, because he knows that the Lord will give him something back. God our heavenly Father demonstrated this. He represents the true example of the Ultimate because He gave us His only begotten Son: "For God so loved the world that he give his one and only Son, that whoever believes in him shall not perish but have eternal life." (John 3:16)

Paul was someone else who, undoubtedly, had reached the Ultimate Stage. Paul could not stop giving thanks to God for the Philippians' Church because he was fully persuaded that God, who had begun good work in them, was also able to complete it. He said:

"I thank my God upon every remembrance of you, always in every prayer of mine making requests for you all with joy, for your fellowship in the Gospel from the first day until now, being confident of this very thing, that He who has begun a good work in you will complete *it* until the day of Jesus Christ." (Philippians 1:3–6)

Paul is convinced that whatever God starts He will complete, because he knows that God is not limited by anything. Paul, therefore, has total confidence in Him. Many people may abandon a project or plan due to a number of reasons: a shortage of resources, lack of skill or the race against time, but God is the provider of all these things and is, therefore, able to fulfil whatever He starts. How persuaded and confident are you when you read God's word? Remember, when you have confidence in God, you also have peace.

I believe that one of the devil's greatest victories over believers is when he succeeds in stopping them from applying the word of God to their daily life and activities. In the context of this book, what I mean by this is when the devil succeeds in preventing believers' progress unto the Ultimate Stage. At the Ultimate Stage, life is transformed by reading, meditating, applying and practising what you have read from the word. It is only through the word of God that success is guaranteed, just as the Lord told Joshua (1:8). When the devil succeeds in stopping somebody from reaching Stage Four – prevents them from reading, meditating, applying and practising the word of God – he has succeed in robbing them of one of the greatest benefits given to them by the Lord.

Knowing that some people will only listen to His word, aware also that some people would only read His word and never bother to obey His word, Jesus told His followers about the benefits of hearing the word and putting into practice His teachings, saying:

(Matthew 7:24) "… everyone who hears these words of mine and puts them into practice is like a wise man who built his house on the rock.

(Matthew 7:25) "Then rain came down, the streams rose, and the winds blew and beat against that house; yet it did not fall, because it had its foundations on the rock.

(Matthew 7:26) "But everyone who hears these words of mine and does not put them into practice is like a foolish man who built his house on sand.

(Matthew 7:27) "The rain came down, the streams rose, and the winds blew and beat against that house; and it fell with great crash."

When you appropriate the word of God into your life, you will be able to withstand any of life's storms; your life will be built on the solid rock of God, which is Christ Jesus.

Unfortunately, the greater number of believers will never reach Stage Four – the Ultimate Stage – during their lifetime, mostly through lack of knowledge in God's word. Most of these people, being so satisfied with the state of having been born again and feeling assured that this alone will ensure them a place in heaven, have become complacent in their striving for the Ultimate, which should not be the case.

Thank God, for those who progress to the Ultimate Stage. They know that, after salvation, all the benefits promised by God to His children here on earth shall also be given to them. Just as Jesus told us: "But seek first the kingdom and his righteousness, and all these things will be given to you as well" (Matthew 6:33). Thus, these people have faith to claim whatever they want from God and receive in return all that He has to offer.

My prayer, therefore, is this: "Dear God may every believer make all efforts to progress to the Ultimate Stage. May they begin to put the word of God into practice in order that they can enjoy all the benefits that God bestowed on us, His children. Amen."

Reading the word of God and failing to put the word into practice or obey its commands is like making a soup, stew or other dish without using any salt. It is like going to see your General Practitioner (GP) or going to hospital, being examined by doctor, given a diagnosis and medicines to cure your sickness, and then failing to take the medicine when you get home. In many ways, I think it's worse if a person even wastes his time visiting the doctor, for you will not get well just by visiting the doctor, you must also do as the doctor has asked. Likewise, when reading the word of God, you must do as God asks you to do, or you have wasted God's time.

Again, because many Christians have failed to progress to the Ultimate Stage, most are greatly lacking, some even more than those in the world (non-believers). Christians who have Christ are supposed to have all things because all things belong to Christ. However, I believe many are struggling because of their failure to believe that whatever they hear, read or preach from the word of God can also work and produce results in their own lives. This doubt puts the devil at a great advantage.

Remember what James instructed: while it is important to read and meditate on God's word, it is even more crucial to obey the word of God and do as it says. No matter in what media you hear, read or preach, what is most important is that you practise the word and are obedient to it. How good it is for a believer to know and believe that the basis of God's word is that one can achieve whatever one desires. Jesus told His disciples and indeed told all believers, saying, "Therefore I tell you, whatever you ask for in prayer, believe that you have received it, and it will be yours." (Mark 11:24)

What I see often, however, is this: instead of Jesus' instruction as I have just quoted, many would like to receive before they believe: they have turned the word of God upside down, which should not be the case, for you must "believe that you have received it."

I believe that for Christians today the most pressing problem or challenge regarding the word of God is not in reading it, or even in witnessing to it, it is practising the word of God, this presents the greatest challenge. True, most believers read or study the word of God and many, after reading or listening to the word, believe what they have read or heard. Some even share what they have studied with others. The problem remains, however, as to how to appropriate what is said in the word so that it is demonstrated by action in life.

How does the believer build the faith to know that the same word as written and read can work for them as an individual, exactly as the Scriptures say it will? They are forgetting what Paul said to the Philippians: "Whatever you have learned or received or heard from me, or seen in me – put it into practice. And the God of peace will be with you." (Philippians 4:9)

Friends, listen to this truth and let it sink into your heart again. No matter how many times you read or preach the word of God to others, appropriating it to your own life is the only way it will make a difference or produce results. For the word of God will do you little good if you don't put it into practice; not even if you put it under your pillow and sleep on it, as is the habit of some! Not even if you swallow it, as I keep saying all the time. You can only benefit by the word by acting on the word: the word of God is not about reading for enjoyment, and so I urge you to act on it now. This is the objective of Stage Four – the Ultimate Stage.

Let me reiterate what I said previously when referring to John and his message to his readers. John knew that only knowing the word of God was not enough and so he instructed that you must do as the word says and you must put the word of God into practice: "Now that you know these things, you will be blessed if you do them." (John 13:17)

If you practice the word of God, your life is secure. If you practice the word of God, your life is built upon the solid rock of Christ Jesus, so nothing can shake it. The word never fails but always produces what it says it will. "For the word of the Lord is right and true; he is faithful in all he does." (Psalm 33:4)

God can be trusted and the Bible, unlike men, is reliable. God does not lie, forget, change His words or leave His promises unfulfilled. We can trust the Bible because it contains the words of a holy, trustworthy and unchangeable God.

Make it your aim and desire to reach the Ultimate Stage, for those at this stage can be secure in the knowledge that God is bound to answer their prayers, and/or come to their aid when acting on His word. As Psalm 138:2 says:

"I will bow down towards your holy temple and will praise your name for your love and your faithfulness, for you have exalted above all things your name and your word."

God, therefore, is always ready to respond and perform exactly as He said He would, just as the Prophet Jeremiah confirmed, "The Lord said to me, 'You have seen correctly for I am watching to see that my word is fulfilled.'" (Jeremiah 1:12)

It has always occurred to me that if God fulfilled all He said He would for Abraham when He (God) swore by His name, then what does he intend to do about all He has said He will do in the Bible knowing that His word is exalted above His name according to Psalm 138:2?

God swears by Himself to bless Abraham
(Genesis 22:15) "The Angel of the Lord called to Abraham from heaven a second time …"

(Genesis 22:16) "… and said, 'I swear by myself,' declares the Lord 'that because you have done this and have not withheld your son, your only son …'

(Genesis 22:17) "… I will surely bless you, and make your descendants as numerous as the stars in the sky and as the sand on the seashore. Your descendants will take possession of the cities of their enemies …

(Genesis 22:18) "… and through your offspring all nations on earth will be blessed, because you have obeyed me."

Until we know, understand and apply the word of God, it will not do us any good even though we may read it, study it or even preach from it. Although God's word has the potential to be life changing, it may not change the life of many. For some, reading the Bible may even become difficult, dull, tedious and even tiring. But when God's word is put into practice it suddenly becomes interesting and enjoyable, this is because we experience the results; the word bears the fruits of our labours.

Those who have reached the Ultimate Stage are also joyful in the knowledge that whatever they pray for will happen. Their prayers are not elementary like those who are babies in the Lord, whose prayers always ask for something. Instead, those at the Ultimate Stage offer praises and worship, thanksgiving, intercession, declaration and decree, knowing that whatever they ask for in prayer will come about, because Jesus said so: "Therefore I tell you, whatever you ask for in prayer, believe that you have received it, and it will be yours." (Mark 11:24)

Let me tell all believers – all those who have progressed from Stage Zero to Stage One and anyone who has been born again – let me tell all of you who have progressed to Stage Two by reading and listening to the word of God and even by preaching or witnessing to others, that if you fail in your attempt to progress to the Ultimate Stage because you do not put into practice that which you read or hear from the Bible then it will be a great loss.

I would say to you that, yes, you will go to heaven but you will miss so many privileges and benefits as a child of God here on earth. To put the word of God into practice is the way to prosperity and success, remember what God told Joshua once again:

"Do not let this Book of the Law depart from your mouth; meditate on it day and night, so that you may be careful to do everything written in it. Then you will be prosperous and successful." (Joshua 1:8)

If you want to enjoy life to the full in God, if you want to enjoy a better relationship with God, if you want to know the heart of God, then begin to put His word into practice. Then you will see the true character of God, and you will know that His word always produces what it says it will.

Jesus said, "Whoever has my commands and obeys them, he is the one who loves me. He who loves me will be loved by my Father, and I too will love him and show myself to him." (John 14:21)

David gave an eloquent description of a person who delights and meditates in the law (the word of God) day and night, saying:

(Psalm 1:1) "Blessed is the man who does not walk in the counsel of the wicked or stand in the way of sinners or sit in the seat of mockers.

(Psalm 1:2) "But his delight is in the law of the Lord, and on his law he meditates day and night.

(Psalm 1:3) "He is like a tree planted by streams of water, which yields its fruit in season and whose leaf does not wither. Whatever he does prospers."

Hold on to the word of God, for all other things are ephemeral. The word of God is everlasting, which is what makes those who have reached the Ultimate Stage so very fortunate and special. For this reason, I pose a challenge to you as you reach this Final Stage in my book: beyond anything else, you may desire to achieve in your life, first ask God's help to reach the Ultimate Stage. To achieve this, you must read, meditate and put into practice the word of God. In this way, you will succeed in all that you pursue, for as the Prophet Isaiah said, "The grass withers and the flowers fall, but the word of our God stands for ever." (Isaiah 40:8)

Even if all things and all people fail you, the word of God will stand solidly by you, for God is always faithful to His word.

RENEWAL OF MIND

Renewing the mind is very important to everyone, irrespective of the stage you belong to, for without the mind renewed a sinner cannot ever be born again. In the same way, one who is born again cannot grow in his newly found faith unless he renews his mind. Also, to become a soul-winner and progress to Stage Four, the Ultimate Stage, one must renew his mind. I always say that the mind is the engine of a person. When one's mind is centred on God and His word, he is safe and secure. It is like a vehicle whose engine is in good condition.

The Psalmist said, "I have set the LORD always before me; because He is at my right hand I shall not be moved." (Psalm 16:8)

Anyone who is able to take control of his mind is in control of his life and his world. At every stage you reach you need to renew your mind, for most things that you have been taught to believe are not biblical, but belong in the tradition of men. The things in which you have been taught to believe have produced fear and disbelief, inferiority complexes, and many other psychological disturbances. These things have made many of people prisoners of themselves, from which they will be freed only by renewal of the mind. I believe, without doubt, that as much as unbelievers at Stage Zero need to change their mind toward God, in the same way, believers also need to change their mind in order to experience God's full blessing in life.

The word 'Renewal' has many meanings depending on how and where it is used. In the context of where I am writing, as far as Romans 12:1–2 is concerned, I would like to use the meaning thus: to replace something that is worn, broken, damaged, expired or no longer suitable for use.

In Romans 12:1–2, Paul said:

"I beseech you therefore, brethren, by the mercies of God, that you present your bodies as a living sacrifice, holy, acceptable to God, which is your reasonable service. And do not be conformed to this world, but be transformed by the renewing of your mind, that you may prove what is that good and acceptable and perfect will of God."

To me verse 1 is the basis for verse 2, therefore, I believe, for a better understanding of verse 2 you must add verse 1. In this quotation, Paul appealed to the believers in Rome to give their bodies to God as a living sacrifice. Before I continue to discuss the living sacrifice part of the letter, let me first share some of the thoughts I had when I read it, for I believe other people may have had the same thought as me. I was wondering why Paul would appeal to the Romans to give their bodies to God as a living sacrifice since God owns their bodies anyway as he later wrote to the church in Corinth, saying:

"Or do you not know that your body is the temple of the Holy Spirit who is in you, whom you have from God, and you are not your own? For you were bought at a price; therefore glorify God in your body and in your spirit, which are God's." (1 Corinthians 6:19–20)

Peter shares the same view with his readers (1 Peter 1:18–19) when he said:

"Knowing that you were not redeemed with corruptible things, *like* silver or gold, from your aimless conduct *received* by tradition from your fathers, but with the precious blood of Christ, as of a lamb without blemish and without spot."

Now, in verse 1 of Romans 12, Paul makes the appeal, which to me means that even though God owns our bodies, still He will not do anything to, or take away anything from man without his (man's) approval, especially when it has to do with life and how it is being lived. This also means that we can still choose to do with our bodies what we want to do, without God interfering.

Paul appeals to the Romans to give their bodies to God as a living sacrifice. In the days of old, sacrificial offerings were very important in the lives of the Israelites.

These offerings were performed when an animal had been killed; the body was placed on the altar and a fire was lit to burn the offering either completely or partially, depending on the type of sacrifice being offered. At this time, the animal has no say in the matter, obviously, because it is dead.

Therefore, Paul's appeal to the Roman believers to give themselves as a living sacrifice means several things. Living, in this context, means to be alive, to exist, as well as expressing something that lives; a living thing should have some say in the outcome of its life. Here, however, Paul suggests to the Romans that they should offer themselves as a dead animal is sacrificed; that is, placed on an altar to burn, as an offering to the Lord.

This sacrifice, Paul says, must also be holy, acceptable to God, "**which** is your reasonable service", he says, which in other words means a spiritual act of worship (Godliness).

In Verse 2, it says, "And do not be conformed to this world, but be transformed by the renewing of your mind, that you may prove what *is* that good and acceptable and perfect will of God."

The first statement means, therefore, that you have offered your body to God as a "living sacrifice, holy, acceptable to God, **which is** your reasonable service or their spiritual act of worship" (Godliness)

He says that after offering yourself, you must not:

1. [Be] conformed to this world, that is, never follow the pattern of the world.

However, he also says that you must:

2. ... be transformed by the renewing of your mind, that is, you must change yourself by the way you think;
3. In doing so, Paul says, you may prove that which is good, acceptable and the perfect will of God.

Two things are clear to me from this reading:

From verse 1 the subject matter is *your* reasonable service, *your* spiritual act of worship" (Godliness).

This can only be achieved by presenting your body as a living sacrifice, holy, and acceptable to God.

The subject of verse 2 is that you may discover what the good, acceptable and perfect will of God is. That is, you may be able to know the perfect will of God in your life. This is only achieved when you do not conform to this world, but rather are transformed by renewal of your mind, which means changing the way you think.

Christians are supposed to be changed persons, mind-renewed people, which Paul reminds us of (2 Corinthians 5:17), saying:

"Therefore, if anyone *is* in Christ, *he is* a new creation; old things have passed away; behold, all things have become new."

It is unfortunate, therefore, that some believers are even worse than unbelievers in the way they think.

Thus, let us now see how we can relate the passage to our personal lives:

1. Reasonable service, the NIV says: "... this is your spiritual act of worship" (Godliness) that comes through living, holy sacrifice acceptable to God.
2. In order to know the perfect will of God we must:

Not conform to this world,

But rather, be transformed by the renewing of your mind.

It is sad, therefore, that many believers, who are supposed to know that we are not of ourselves and that our bodies belong to God, act childishly, like children, and refuse to give up their bodies to serve God, even though He owns us as we learnt earlier on. We are all servants of God.

I would be interested to know whether you feel anguish, if you have ever given food or cookies to a child, and then when you turn to beg him or her to give you some, she or he refuses to give you any, even sometimes crying because you asked him or her for a morsel. This is the effect we have on God when we refuse to give ourselves to Him.

Another point of interest is that in verse 1, which is about failing to offer one's body as a living and holy sacrifice, the point is reiterated, because if one fails in the first point, one automatically fails the second; that of knowing the perfect will of God, which is learnt by not conforming to this world and worldly things.

Rather become transformed by renewing your mind. Because when one fails to give or surrender his life to God, he cannot think the way God thinks, that is, according to His word.

One must resist conforming to the pattern of the world, but instead renew one's mind to achieve transformation. This comes about through the word of God, which is also God's will.

How can one renew his mind? The mind can only be renewed when one is willing to do exactly as God's word says we should do. For example, the world will say my body is mine and I can do anything with it; but the word of God will say my body belongs to God. Another example, the world will say going to church is waste of time, and giving to God is even worse; but the word of God will say the opposite.

Paul said (1 Timothy 6:6) that it is a great gain when we give or devote ourselves to God. He said:

"Now godliness (reasonable service or worship) with contentment is great gain."

David knew that it is only through the word of God that one can faithfully serve the Lord, he said:

"How can a young man cleanse his way? By taking heed according to Your word. With my whole heart, I have sought You; Oh, let me not wander from Your commandments! Your word I have hidden in my heart that I might not sin against You!" (Psalm 119:9–11)

Renew your mind with the word of God, which has the power to transform anything or anybody, and you will be able to take control of your life. Paul said,

"I am not ashamed of the gospel, because it is the power of God for the salvation of everyone who believes: first for the Jew, then for the Gentile." (Romans 1:16)

He also said this about the word when he wrote to the Colossians Church:

"This same Good News that came to you is going out all over the world. It is changing lives everywhere, just as it changed yours that very first day you heard and understood the truth about God's great kindness to sinners." (Colossians 1:6)

CONCLUSION

In conclusion, after you have spent hours, maybe days, reading this book, I want to ask you one very important and searching question:

Where do you belong?

Do you find yourself still at Stage Zero, in darkness, totally separated from God and doomed to hell?

Are you at Stage One, having repented, or have you been born again?

Are you at Stage Two, growing in the knowledge of God? Or are you still feeding on baby's milk?

Are you at Stage Three, responding to the Great Commission, winning souls for Christ?

Or have you reached Stage Four, the Ultimate Stage, having not only passed through the first three stages, but also now reading the word of God, meditating on what you read day and night, and obeying it? Are you precisely doing all that you read, and practising all that you know?

You must definitely find yourself at one of these stages, for no one can avoid all of the stages. Note that if you are still at Stage Zero you are heading towards hell, everlasting suffering, and eternal death and separation from the Lord. If that is the case, why wait until it is too late? Why head for hell when the freely given Son of God, Jesus Christ, who gave Himself for our sins, to rescue us from the present evil age, according to the will of our God and Father, is waiting to save and reconnect you to God His Father?

By God's grace, for those of us who have progressed from Stage Zero to Stage One, I will say to you also that this is not all: you must continue to work out your salvation with fear and trembling (Philippians 2:12), knowing that there is more room for growth in your relationship with God.

There are benefits that come about only by reading, believing and practising the word of God. Let me ask you the following questions:

Do you read the word of God?
Do you believe what you read?
Do you share what you read with others?
Do you practice what you read?

If your answer to any of the questions above is "No", then I urge you, please put things right before it is too late.

Always remember what God told Joshua:
"Do not let this Book of the Law depart from your mouth; meditate on it day and night, so that you may be careful to do everything written in it. Then you will be prosperous and successful." (Joshua 1:8) this is the key to success and prosperity in every area of life.

It is my heart's desire and the answer to my prayer that you will come to know Christ after reading this book. Let me appeal to you all: if you are a non-believer, understand that hell and eternal death await you and anyone who does not believe in Jesus Christ the Son of God, the only mediator between God and Man.

"This is good, and pleases God our Saviour, who wants all men to be saved and to come to knowledge of the truth. For there is one God, and one mediator between God and men, the man Christ Jesus, who gave himself as a ransom for all men – the testimony given in its proper time." (1 Timothy 2:3–6)

To those who know Him already let me remind you that Jesus Christ is not only our Saviour but our Lord as well. Make every effort, therefore, to obey His Commandments and take responsibility in sharing His word with others.

If you have progressed from Stage Zero congratulations. This step represents the greatest move you have made or will ever make in your entire life. However,

I urge you not to stay put there: persevere and move on until you reach the Ultimate Stage, where you will always read, meditate and practise the word of God. This will help you to make your way to prosperity and success.

Luke tells believers in the Book of Acts that their knowledge in God's word will lead them to their inheritance. This means that your knowledge, understanding and practise of the word of God will reveal to you one thing: that all things are there for those who are in Christ Jesus, for they will lack nothing.

"Now I commit you to God and to the word of his grace, which can build you up and give you an inheritance among all those who are sanctified." (Acts 20:32)

Paul also said, "So then, no more boasting about men! All things are yours." (1 Corinthians 3:21)

In the Psalm it says:

"The unfolding of your words gives light; it gives understanding to the simple." (Psalm 119:130)

"The law of the Lord is perfect, reviving the soul. The statutes of the Lord are trustworthy, making wise the simple. The precepts of the Lord are right, giving joy to the heart. The commands of the Lord are radiant, giving light to the eyes. The fear of the Lord is pure, enduring for ever. The ordinances of the Lord are sure and altogether righteous. They are more precious than gold, than much pure gold: they are sweeter than honey, than honey from the comb. By them is your servant warned; in keeping them there is great reward." (Psalm 19:7–11)

Before I put down my pen, let me say to you again, if you are a non-believer, a candidate of Stage Zero, and you have had the opportunity to read this book, I pray that you realise that this is your opportune time, the day of your salvation! The Lord wants you to know the truth and get on the path that leads to eternal life, because as the word of God says, "He wishes that none would perish but everyone to come to repentance." (2 Peter 3:8–9)

To my fellow believers I say to you, this book is a call to action for you, a time to grow, a time to share your faith with others with the aim to bring them to Christ for them to be saved. It is your opportunity too, to enjoy a higher relationship with God by reading, meditating and practising the word of God. If you do that, you will succeed and prosper in everything you do.

Finally, may God richly bless you for taking the time to read *Be Ye Transformed: The Steps to Spiritual Transformation*, which I believe will bring about a great transformation to your spiritual and physical life. May the Lord be with you and grant you success in everything you do. Amen.

Other Publications by

Pastor David Amoah

Temptation

Stay Connected to Christ

Your Future Is In Your Hand

The Power For Your Zero Hour

Guidelines For Preachers and Teachers of God's Word

The Favour of God: Discovering God's Hidden Treasure

CONTACT DETAILS

For more copies of this book and other publications by Pastor David Amoah; to make an appointment for preaching or teaching; for prayer, support and counselling, please contact:

The Good Way Apostolic Church office

110-118 Markfield Road

London N15 4QF

T: 020 8801 4298, **Mob:** 07575230988

E: amoahdla@yahoo.co.uk |

W: www.davidamoah.co.uk

www.ingramcontent.com/pod-product-compliance
Lightning Source LLC
Chambersburg PA
CBHW071232080526
44587CB00013BA/1574